Contemporary Discourse
in the Field of
BIOLOGY™

Biological Evolution

An Anthology
of Current Thought

Edited by Katy Human

The Rosen Publishing Group, Inc., New York

Published in 2006 by The Rosen Publishing Group, Inc.
29 East 21st Street, New York, NY 10010

First Edition

Library of Congress Cataloging-in-Publication Data

Biological evolution : an anthology of current thought /
edited by Katy Human.— 1st ed.
 p. cm. — (Contemporary discourse in the field of biology)
Includes bibliographical references and index.
ISBN 1-4042-0403-2 (lib. bdg.)
1. Evolution (Biology)—Juvenile literature.
I. Human, Katy. II. Series.
QH367.1.B54 2005
576.8—dc22

                                        2004027346

Manufactured in the United States of America

On the cover: Bottom right: The 3.3 million-year-old bones
from the *Austalopithecus afarensis* hominid nicknamed "Lucy,"
the earliest known ancestor of humans. Top: Digital cell. Far
left: Digital cell. Bottom left: Austrian monk and botanist
Gregor Johann Mendel (1822–1884).

CONTENTS

Introduction

Giant dinosaurs once ambled across a field of mud in what is now a remote part of south-eastern Colorado. It was not easy to get to the Purgatoire River canyon in the late fall or early spring. The hard slog through mud and snow was worth it, however, because ice formed in the hundreds of fossilized dinosaur footprints along the river's edge. Pry the ice out, and you are holding a frozen mold of an ancient creature's foot in your hand—a perfectly preserved record of evolution.

We humans are fascinated with evolution for many reasons. Some of us want to learn about where we came from, our origins as a species. Others want to understand how we are related to the millions of other fascinating organisms with which we share the planet or which were here before we were and are now extinct. Still others wonder why we look the way we do, why we fall in (and out of) love, and become ill in the ways we do. Evolution does not have all the answers to these questions, but it invariably has insight to offer and some fascinating hypotheses grounded in hard science and empirical research.

Evolution can be described with a seven-word phrase: genetic change, over time, within a population. Of course, evolution is far more complicated than this definition suggests, and researchers often spend decades studying just one tiny subcategory of this enormous field. One evolutionary biologist might focus on fossils from 500 million years ago found in northern Alberta, in western Canada. Another might devise and run elaborate computer programs designed to mimic the complex processes of natural selection, offering clues to how life has evolved over time and what future adaptations may lie ahead.

Evolutionary biologists are fundamentally interested in the forces that shape organisms, such as the evolutionary and genetic arms race between predator and prey that pushes each to become ever faster or more clever or better defended. The competition among members of a species for mates that can lead to seemingly extreme and outlandish behavior, from ritualized fighting and ostentatious bower building to cocky strutting, is also an enduring source of interest among evolutionary biologists. Evolutionary "accidents"—or mutations—are an especially fascinating, occasionally even urgent, field of study, because these accidents change the course of history. For example, genetic drift, the random or accidental mutation of genes, may leave a population vulnerable to deadly disease. The study of evolution, therefore, is not merely academic or undertaken to satisfy curiosity; sometimes it is part of a life-or-death search for knowledge.

In this anthology of leading, cutting-edge scholarship on biological evolution, you will read about how natural selection has camouflaged the coats of rodents in the American Southwest and may or may not have changed the coloring of peppered moths in response to the soot and smog produced in England during the Industrial Revolution. You will learn about the myriad ways humans tamper with the evolutionary process, through pollution, climate change, selective breeding and grafting, and genetic engineering. Some of these essays showcase the new tools scientists are using to probe the fundamentals of evolution. These tools include gene sequencing, which helps us understand DNA differences between related organisms, as well as sophisticated computer models with which scientists can "replay" the tape of evolution.

Many potentially revolutionary ideas are presented here, some of which may prove over the course of time to be flawed, while others may transform the science of evolution. Niche construction is one example: some evolutionary biologists now believe that by altering environments, organisms change the force of natural selection itself. Rather than always being acted upon by their environment and adapting to it, organisms can alter their surroundings and set in motion ripples of evolutionary responses. Some biologists even believe that organisms may be able to control the "throttle" of evolution, slowing or speeding its pace depending on the amount of environmental stress placed upon them. They may "save" genetic mutations for difficult periods—drought, cold, famine—when they most need to adapt to extreme conditions or sudden habitat, climate, or environmental changes.

It is impossible to predict with certainty which new theories will bear fruit and which will eventually be discredited. One of the appeals of evolution is that it seems to have something interesting and revelatory to say about every element in the natural world. For example, why do crabs scuttle so strangely? Evolutionary biologists would probably argue that the crab's nonlinear, unpredictable path is a defensive adaptation that allows it to confuse predators and avoid being eaten. Such hypotheses are worth developing, but they remain "just so" stories until they are put to the test, a neat and tidy way to explain away mystery. Evolution is a science, after all, and its theories must be subject to the rigors of objective, empirical research and experimentation.

The problem is that science is neither monolithic nor etched in stone. There is good science, bad science, and mediocre science, depending on the quality of the minds and methods of the men and women who engage in it. Conventional scientific wisdom is also far from immutable, shifting and changing with each century, each generation, each new study. Science can also be hopelessly compromised by the prejudices and preconceived notions of researchers, who, after all, are only flawed humans like the rest of us. In the nineteenth century, for example, some so-called scientists argued that people of African descent were less evolved than people of northern European descent. The "proof" lay in facial angles—the prominent chins of Europeans were thought to be related to intelligence. There is no such relationship, of course, and it was evolutionary biologists who helped to expose these race-based theories as utter nonsense. These biologists discovered that the chin is actually just an evolutionary accident, a mere by-product of stress and growth in the human jawbone.

A further source of uncertainty and complication regarding the validity of any given evolutionary theory is that, contrary to popular belief, evolution is not the same thing as progress. A given adaptation may be one solution to a certain problem that a species must solve in order to survive, but that does not mean it is necessarily the only or the best solution. Most adaptations simply get the job done, but they don't represent a milestone on the road to some kind of physical perfection. Because evolution is not the same thing as progress, analyzing past adaptations and predicting the future is a complicated and inexact science.

Just as evolution is not necessarily progress, so, too, are humans not standing at the pinnacle of existence, the supreme end result of evolutionary forces. By no measure are humans any more "evolved" than any other organism alive today. The bacteria on our skin and mites in our eyebrows have "figured out" their own ways to thrive, just as *Homo sapiens* has. Those old diagrams showing a progression of animals walking out of the water onto land, from fish to four-legged amphibian to monkey to

human, are deceptive and inaccurate. In evolutionary terms, bacteria, by some accounts, are actually far more successful than humans: they are more diverse, more numerous, and, in many cases, far more powerful than we are. Even with the help of our expensive medicines and high-tech medical industry, some of these bacteria can kill us. Bacteria also have a ruthlessly effective way of rapidly evolving to defeat almost any medicine we develop to fight them.

Uncertainty, randomness, nonlinearity, and lack of hierarchy seem to rule existence, at least where evolution is concerned. The old, discredited equation of evolution with progress has been largely superseded by the almost whimsical notion that evolution requires mistakes to bring about specieswide adaptation. Natural selection requires variation, and variation requires mutations—those accidental deletions or additions of material deep within the DNA of our cells. In an increasingly slick, fast-paced, automated, impersonal world, one in which we are constantly being reminded of the narrow margin for error, it is refreshing to be reminded that mistakes are a powerful and necessary creative force. A few important but subtle "mistakes," in evolutionary terms, may save the human race. —KH

The Basic Mechanics of Evolution

It has long been believed that many species formed through allopatric speciation. That is, separate species developed due to geographic separation or isolation. Imagine a river or a mountain range splitting a population of organisms into two geographically distinct camps. It is now easy to imagine how those two separated populations might diverge over time. Some species may have formed that way, biologists acknowledge, but more and more, researchers are finding evidence that it is sympatric speciation—the separate evolutionary development of a once-unified population existing within the same environment and geographic region—that may be far more prevalent. In this article, Ian Stewart uses mathematics to explain sympatric speciation. He comes up with a surprising conclusion: mathematically, it is not at all difficult to make two species from one. In fact, speciation is, put simply, "how the world works," he writes. Stewart compares speciation to physical processes that exhibit "symmetry-breaking" behavior. Stress a "symmetric system"—a thin rod of uniform metal, for example—and the symmetry will eventually break. If subjected to enough physical stress, a metal rod will eventually bend, then break. In biology, if a collection of nearly uniform individuals and different groups is subjected to stress, separate species will begin to emerge. Since stress is nearly inevitable in the natural world—droughts, floods, food shortages, predation—so, too, is speciation. —KH

"How the Species Became"
by Ian Stewart
New Scientist, October 11, 2003

One of the ironies of Charles Darwin's *On The Origin of Species* is that while it provides ample evidence that new species evolve from existing ones, it doesn't tell us much about how it happens. It is easy to see that natural selection can cause a species to change as time passes, but it is much less clear why a single species should split into two distinct branches of the evolutionary tree. If some external change makes certain members of a population more able to survive than others, then surely that change will make the whole species evolve in that direction. How could two separate species emerge from one?

Speciation is a complex business, taking place over vastly different scales of size and time. There is no reason to suppose that it is governed by just one force—after all, we know that genetic mutations and sexual recombination of existing genes vie with environmental influences, depletion of resources, parasites, migration and disease. But although many theories and ideas have been offered up to account for speciation, it remains one of the big puzzles in biology.

Within the flurry of activity that surrounds this conundrum there are two very noticeable trends. One is a shift of focus away from theories in which species formation occurs as the direct result of major environmental and geographic differences. The new focus is on situations where speciation takes place without any dramatic changes, in a single interbreeding population of very similar creatures, all in much the same environment. Nearly all publications on speciation in *Nature* and *Science* over the past five years or so focus on this undramatic scenario—a complete reversal of what used to be the case.

The other trend is the growing use of mathematical models, a technique more usually employed to explore aspects of physics. These models are being used by myself and others to describe the natural dynamics of speciation. And when applied to the "undramatic" instances of speciation, they have produced some very interesting results.

The maths indicates that far from being a surprising phenomenon, it would be very odd if speciation didn't occur. It appears to be a result of exactly the same process that filled the universe with matter, creating subatomic particles, planets, sand dunes and—ultimately—humans. Strange as it may seem, neutrons, narwhals, electrons and elephants in some way seem to owe their diverse characteristics to a principle that dictates much of what happens in the physical world.

That principle is known to physicists and mathematicians as "symmetry-breaking." An example is the formation of sand dunes. Reducing it to its mathematical ideal, a uniform wind blowing across a uniform desert will produce parallel ridges of sand. The featureless desert had all the symmetries of a flat plane: rotate it through any angle and it will look the same. The wind, however, reduces the level of symmetry: the parallel ridges of the dunes introduce a definite direction, or orientation, into the landscape.

Such symmetry-breaking happens naturally all over the place. For example, if you heat a flat dish of fluid uniformly from below, at a certain critical temperature the uniformity is broken by the onset of a complex pattern of convection cells. They are typically hexagonal, with a few pentagons thrown in, and all much the same size. As with the formation of sand dunes, the symmetry breaks down, in this case reducing to the symmetries of a roughly hexagonal lattice.

Filling the Universe

On a far grander scale, physicists believe a type of symmetry-breaking was responsible for the formation of subatomic particles from the fields that filled the primordial universe. These particles are, of course, the building blocks of matter, so you could argue that symmetry-breaking helped create pretty much everything that exists.

But what does symmetry-breaking have to do with speciation? Although the commonest definition of "same species" in sexual populations has been "able to interbreed," biologists have been seeking an alternative definition for some time, because there are too many cases in which this one just doesn't fit. In a paper published in *BioEssays* this year (vol 25, p 596), Massimo Pigliucci of the University of Tennessee in Knoxville analysed nine well-known definitions of "species," and found serious problems with them all.

So instead of chasing a formal definition of species, biologists are going back to the more intuitive idea that organisms belong to the same species if they are effectively indistinguishable. The degree of similarity can be quantified by listing anatomical or behavioural features and observing how closely they match. And this is where symmetry comes in.

The symmetry of an object or system is simply a transformation that preserves its structure. With speciation, the transformations are not rotations or flips, as with the symmetries of a sphere or a hexagon, but permutations—shufflings of the labels employed in the model to identify the individual organisms.

A group of 10 identical objects possesses a symmetry: line them up and turn your back for a moment, and you wouldn't know if any or all of them switched position in the line. But if the line were composed of five objects that had one shape followed by five that had another, some of the symmetry is broken: swapping numbers 5 and 6 around, for instance, would produce an obvious change. From this point of view, the definition of a species is simply that it is symmetric, and speciation is then just a form of symmetry-breaking. With this definition in place, mathematicians and physicists can apply their existing theory of symmetry-breaking. This describes how, why and when a given group of symmetries will typically break up into subgroups—species, in this case.

Biologists traditionally recognise two distinct types of speciation. The first is "allopatric" ("different family") speciation, in which some major geographical change splits a population in two. Once separated, the two groups evolve independently, eventually changing so much that they become two distinct species. Even if reunited, they remain distinct species.

The second is "sympatric," or same-family speciation, in which new species emerge without separation. You might think that mating between neighbouring animals would encourage "gene flow"—the mixing of "alleles" or gene alternatives that occurs when individuals mate—and would tend to keep the gene pool homogeneous. Classically, this was interpreted as keeping it a single species. But it seems this isn't always the case. Examples include the recent discovery that there are two species of African elephant, and the 13 species of finch on the Galapagos Islands, which helped set Darwin on the road to what he called "the mutability of species."

Until around the mid-1990s, allopatric speciation was thought to be by far the most common, but biologists now seem to have begun shifting their view: sympatric speciation, though subtle and counter-intuitive, may be the more important mechanism. The homogenising gene flow within a species can be disrupted by many things: geography is just the most obvious. And that's exactly what the mathematical analysis of speciation seems to be suggesting.

The mathematical picture of speciation highlights at least three "universal" phenomena—rules, almost. The first is that when a population first speciates, it usually splits into precisely two distinguishable types. To see three or more new species is a rare, mainly transitory phenomenon. The second is that the split occurs very rapidly in the population—much faster than the usual rate of noticeable changes in characteristics, or phenotype. So, for example, a significant change in beak length might happen within a few generations, rather than by tiny increments over many generations. The third phenomenon is that the two new species will evolve in opposite directions: if one evolves larger beaks, the other will evolve smaller ones.

So what causes that initial split? Our knowledge of symmetry-breaking in physics suggests that a key step is the onset of some kind of instability in the population. An example in physics would be a stick being bent by stronger and stronger forces: something suddenly gives way and the stick snaps in two. Why? Because the two-part state is stable, whereas one over-stressed stick is not. The loss of symmetry is rapid—and irreversible.

The symmetry-breaking models for speciation do indeed indicate that instability can be a trigger. To be precise about it, a species is called "stable" if small changes in form or behaviour tend to be damped out in subsequent generations. It is unstable if they grow out of control as new generations shuffle the genes of their parents and natural selection discards combinations that don't work so well.

Speciation models show that if you subject a population to subtle, gradual changes in environmental or population pressures, it can suddenly cross a threshold from stable to unstable. At that point, all hell breaks loose. As the environment or population size changes, the single-species state may cease to be stable, so that if by chance a few birds diverge from the average phenotype, the divergence grows instead of damping down. The result is that small, random disturbances can lead to big changes.

Thanks to tiny, random variations that occur naturally—in, say, the beak sizes of a population of finches—anything that changes the characteristics of the food supply even slightly can bestow an advantage on birds with slightly above or below average beak size. The mathematical analysis shows that once the balance swings in favour of avoiding the middle ground, there is a collective pressure that rapidly drives the birds into two distinct types that don't compete directly for food. Instead, they avoid competition by exploiting distinct niches. This demolishes the argument that the whole population ought to evolve in the same direction, and it opens the door to species divergence in a uniform, interbreeding population.

Either of these clumps may split again later, as continuing changes to the environment change the availability of resources. Such a sequence of sympatric splittings is probably how the original single finch species on the Galapagos Islands became 13 (or 14, counting one further species on the Cocos Islands).

The model I have talked about is highly simplified: all creatures in the given species are identical. But researchers are working to remove this crude approximation. One approach is simply to add "random noise" to the equations, so that the phenotype (body-plan and behaviour) passes from generation to generation as per the original rules, but plus or minus small random variations. In this scenario, a population corresponds to a cluster of organisms in phenotypic "space"—an abstract space whose "coordinates" might be beak size, wing span, and so on—rather than a single point. Interestingly, we have found that the clumps split up in much the same way that the original points divided, but the noise makes speciation happen a little more easily.

An even more intriguing approach is to use the original noise-free equations but to modify them so that at each generation the creatures mate according to a set of randomly chosen pairings. In this scenario, all variation is caused by mating. Again, what we see is clusters, not single points, but these clumps are tighter than in the random noise model, since the homogenising gene flow pulls the population closer together, just as Harvard zoologist Ernst Mayr has argued it should.

Birds of a Feather

But contrary to what Mayr thought, divergent splits can still occur, and when they do a tight clump diverges into two much looser ones. After that, even though the creatures can choose mates from the other group, the clusters tighten up and remain separate from each other. This behaviour is not fully understood even mathematically (though curiously it appears to be related to fractal geometry), but it seems very close to what happens in real populations. All the same, we can see that sympatric speciation is not as surprising as we first thought.

This kind of modelling is still in its infancy. Its main achievement so far is to show that sympatric speciation is entirely reasonable and natural, and to focus attention on the role of instability as a mechanism for speciation. Species become unstable when small but critical changes to their common environment—what food is available, for example—make new gene combinations superior to the existing ones. This alone can cause the phenotypes to rapidly diverge, and contrary to what many textbooks say, it doesn't require mutations within the DNA code. The population just shuffles its existing genes into new arrangements.

Work is already under way to make the models more biologically realistic in order to give a deeper understanding of the nature of these instabilities. My University of Warwick colleague, mathematician Toby Elmhirst, has modelled finch speciation, for instance. His research follows work done in 1999 by Ulf

Dieckmann of the International Institute for Applied Systems Analysis in Laxenburg, Austria, and Michael Doebeli of the University of Basel. The approach may tell us about the effect of non-uniform habitat—allopatry as well as sympatry, or subtle mixtures like patchy environments—and it can model sexual and asexual reproduction. The result may yield new insights into how evolution has occurred in the past by placing more emphasis on the links between phenotype and habitat.

Another major objective is to incorporate genetics explicitly. At the moment, its role is implicit: it simply lets the phenotype change. It would be a huge achievement to establish the link between the detailed genetic changes and the phenotypic ones. Such breakthroughs may come from work being carried out by other groups, such as those of Eva Kisdi and Stefan Geritz of the University of Turku in Finland. Their method, known as "adaptive dynamics," follows the same general line of thought as ours, but uses markedly different models. It focuses on the genes in very much the same way we focus on phenotype, and their results give insights into the forces behind allopatric speciation (*Evolution*, vol 53, p 993). The two approaches seem very complementary, and I hope (and expect) that they will join forces as the subject unfolds.

In the meantime, we can at least say that the symmetry-breaking approach puts the whole problem in a new light. Species diverge because of an unmanageable loss of stability. The actual sequence of events—which gene does what, and in what order—determines the precise response to this loss of stability, but it depends on a bewildering variety of accidental factors, such as which birds get the bigger beaks and which get the smaller ones. Broadly speaking, such details are less important than the overall context. They may appear to be the causes of speciation, but actually they are just the effects of a far-reaching instability. An over-stressed stick must break. An over-stressed group of birds must either speciate or die. Speciation is not surprising—it is simply how the world works.

Reprinted with permission from *New Scientist*.

Impatient with the ongoing illogical and often politically motivated debate over evolution versus creationism, the authors of this article attempt to leave the debate behind altogether and proclaim that evolution is no longer just a theory. It is cold, hard reality, and it is occurring all around us, all the time, as "real as hunger and as unavoidable as death," the authors write. And while evolution rarely seems to produce the best possible solution to any given problem faced by an organism, it almost always provides a solution that works. Putting evolution to work for the good of all is a particular concern of the authors. Scientists today must have a sure understanding of evolutionary processes if they are ever to prevent and cure diseases that kill millions of people every year. Two particularly

deadly and prevalent diseases are malaria and AIDS. Because both the parasite that causes malaria and the virus that leads to AIDS evolve and mutate very quickly and aggressively, they soon "outwit" many of the drugs we develop to fight them. Do you want to find a cure for AIDS? Study evolution, these writers exhort. —KH

"A Theory Evolves"
by Thomas Hayden, Jessica Ruvinsky, Dan Gilgoff, and Rachel K. Sobel
U.S. News and World Report, July 29, 2002

When scientists introduced the world to humankind's earliest known ancestor two weeks ago, they showed us more than a mere museum piece. Peering at the 7 million-year-old skull is almost like seeing a reflection of our earlier selves. And yet that fossil represents only a recent chapter in a grander story, beginning with the first single-celled life that arose and began evolving some 3.8 billion years ago. Now, as the science of evolution moves beyond guesswork, we are learning something even more remarkable: how that tale unfolded.

Scientists are uncovering the step-by-step changes in form and function that ultimately produced humanity and the diversity of life surrounding us. By now, scientists say, evolution is no longer "just a theory." It's an everyday phenomenon, a fundamental fact of biology as real as hunger and as unavoidable as death.

Darwin proposed his theory of evolution based on extensive observations and cast-iron logic. Organisms produce more young than can survive, he noted, and when random changes create slight differences between offspring, "natural selection" tends to kill off those that are less well suited to the environment. But Darwin's evidence was fragmentary, and with the science of genetics yet to be invented, he was left without an explanation for how life might actually change.

The "modern synthesis" of genetics and evolutionary theory in the 1940s began to fill that gap. But until recently, much of evolution still felt to nonscientists like abstract theory, often presented in ponderous tomes like paleontologist Stephen Jay Gould's 1,464-page *Structure of Evolutionary Theory*, published shortly before his death this spring. As theorists argued over arcane points and creationists stressed uncertainties to challenge evolution's very reality, many people were left confused, unsure what to believe.

Nuts and Bolts

But away from heated debates in schools and legislatures, a new generation of scientists has been systematically probing the fossil record, deciphering genomes, and scrutinizing the details of plant and animal development. They are documenting how evolution actually worked, how it continues to transform our world, and even how we can put it to work to fight disease and analyze the wealth of data from genome-sequencing projects. "The big story," says evolutionary biologist E. O. Wilson of Harvard University, "is not in overarching, top-down theory now, but in the details of research in the lab and in the field."

Scientists have confirmed virtually all of Darwin's postulates. For example, Ward Watt of Stanford University has demonstrated natural selection in action. In a hot environment, he found, butterflies with a heat-stable form of a metabolic gene outreproduced their cousins with a form that works well only at lower temperatures. "Darwin was more right than he knew," says Watt. Darwin also held that new species evolve slowly, the result of countless small changes over many generations, and he attributed the lack of transitional forms—missing links—to the spotty nature of the fossil record. By now many gaps have been filled. Dinosaur researchers can join hands with bird experts, for example, their once disparate fields linked by a series of fossils that show dinosaurs evolving feathers and giving rise to modern birds. And last year, paleontologists announced that they had recovered fossils from the hills of Pakistan showing, step by step, how hairy, doglike creatures took to the sea and became the first whales.

But new research also shows that evolution works in ways Darwin did not imagine. Many creatures still appear quite suddenly in the fossil record, and the growing suspicion is that evolution sometimes leaps, rather than crawls. For example, the first complex animals, including worms, mollusks, and shrimplike arthropods, show up some 545 million years ago; paleontologists have searched far and wide for fossil evidence of gradual progress toward these advanced creatures but have come up empty. "Paleontologists have the best eyes in the world," says Whitey Hagadorn of Amherst College, who has scoured the rocks of the

Southwest and California for signs of the earliest animal life. "If we can't find the fossils, sometimes you have to think that they just weren't there."

A new understanding of Earth's history helps explain why. Scientists have learned that our planet has been rocked periodically by catastrophes: enormous volcanic eruptions that belched carbon dioxide, creating a super greenhouse effect; severe cold spells that left much of the planet enveloped in ice; collisions with asteroids. These convulsions killed off much of life's diversity. Once conditions improved, says Harvard paleontologist Andy Knoll, the survivors found a world of new opportunities. They were freed to fill new roles, "experimenting" with new body plans and evolving too rapidly to leave a record in the fossils.

We may owe our own dominance to the asteroid impact that killed the dinosaurs 65 million years ago. As mammals, we like to think that we're pretty darned superior. The sad truth: "Mammals coexisted with dinosaurs for 150 million years but were never able to get beyond little ratlike things," says Knoll. "It was only when the dinosaurs were removed that mammals had the ecological freedom to evolve new features."

Whether evolution worked fast or slow, theorists labored to explain how it could produce dramatic changes in body structure through incremental steps. Half an eye would be worse than none at all, creationists were fond of arguing. But "partial" eyes turn out to be common in nature, and biologists can trace eye evolution from the lensless flatworm eyespot to the complex geometry of vertebrate eyes. Now "evo-devo" biologists, who study how fertilized egg cells develop into adults, are discovering powerful new ways evolution can transform organisms. They are finding that changes in a handful of key genes that control development can be enough to drastically reshape an animal.

Master Switches

The central discovery of evo-devo is that the development and ultimate shape of animal bodies are orchestrated by a small set of genes called homeotic genes. These regulatory genes make proteins that act as master switches. By binding to DNA, they turn on or shut down other genes that actually make tissues. All but the simplest animals are built in segments (most obvious in creatures like centipedes, but also apparent in human vertebrae), and the Hox family of homeotic genes interacts to determine what each segment will look like. By simple genetic tinkering, evo-devo biologists can tweak the controls, making flies with legs where their antennae should be, or eyeballs on their knees.

This might seem like little more than a cruel parlor trick, and the resulting monstrosities would never survive in nature. But small changes in these master-switch genes may help explain some major changes in evolutionary history. This past winter, evo-devo biologists showed that an important animal transition 400 million years ago, when many-legged arthropods (think lobsters) gave rise to six-legged insects, was due to just a few mutations in a Hox gene. In the past few months, researchers have found that a change in the regulation of a growth-factor gene could have resulted in the first vertebrate jaw. And, incredibly, researchers reported in the journal *Science* last week that a single mutation in a regulatory gene was enough to produce mice with brains that had an unusually large, wrinkled cerebral cortex resembling our own. (No word, though, on whether the mutant mice gained smarts.)

Some critics of evolution argue that animals are so complex and their parts so interconnected that any change big enough to produce a new species would cause fatal failures. Call it the Microsoft conundrum. But just as Judge Thomas Penfield Jackson managed to delete that company's Web browser on his own computer without crashing the operating system, evo-devo biologists are learning how evolution can tweak one part of an animal while leaving everything else alone. The key to modifying the machine of life while it's running, says biologist Sean Carroll of the University of Wisconsin-Madison, is mutations in the stretches of DNA that homeotic proteins bind to.

"If you change a Hox protein, you might mess up the whole body," says Carroll. "But if you change a control element, you can change a part as small as a bristle or a fingernail." He explains that genetic accidents can set the stage by duplicating segments, creating spares that are free to evolve while the other segments carry on with their original function. Biologists now believe that appendages like insect wings and the proboscis a mosquito jabs you with evolved from spare leg segments.

Making Do

This process may be rapid, but it's not elegant. Instead of inventing new features from scratch, evolution works with what it has, modifying existing structures by trial and error. The result is a messy legacy of complicated biochemical pathways and body parts that are more serviceable than sleekly designed. Although proponents of intelligent design hold that organisms are too "perfect" to have arisen by chance, science shows that organisms don't work perfectly at all; they just work.

While many scientists busy themselves figuring out the history and mechanics of evolution, others are already putting it to use. Jonathan Eisen of the Institute for Genomic Research in Rockville, Md., deciphers the information stored in organisms' genomes for clues to their ancestry and how they function. For him, evolution is as critical a tool as DNA-sequencing machines and supercomputers. "If I didn't approach everything with an evolutionary perspective," says Eisen, "I'd miss out on most of the information."

That's because genomes are the handiwork of evolution, and their origin can be key to making sense of them. Researchers analyzing the human genome, for example, reported finding a series of human genes that were also common in bacteria but absent from invertebrates like fruit flies. They concluded that bacterial genes had infiltrated vertebrate animals, helping to shape our genetic identity. But the explanation turned out to be more mundane. Knowing how evolution often prunes away unneeded genes, Eisen and several others showed most of the suspect genes had simply been dropped during the evolutionary history of flies. The moral of the story: "I'm begging people to treat evolution as a science and not just tack it on as an explanation afterwards," says Eisen.

Arms Race

For microbiologist Richard Lenski, evolution is an obvious reality. Since 1988, the Michigan State University professor has been following 12 populations of the bacterium E. coli. With a new generation every 3.5 hours or so, this is evolution on fast-forward. The populations were once genetically identical, but each has adapted in its own way to the conditions in its test-tube home. The same speedy adaptation, unfortunately, can be readily seen in hospitals, where powerful antibiotics provide a major selective advantage for bacteria that evolve resistance. As bacterial evolution outwits one antibiotic after another, notes Harvard evolutionary biologist Stephen Palumbi, treating infections has become an evolutionary arms race. "It's a cycle of escalation, and the entity that can make the last turn of the cycle wins," says Palumbi. "So far, there's no indication that it's going to be us." The answer, he says, is not just new antibiotics but new strategies based on evolution.

"The key is to tip the balance of selection in favor of mild organisms," says evolutionary biologist Paul Ewald of Amherst College. That can mean measures as simple as having doctors scrub their hands to prevent the spread of the dangerous, antibiotic-resistant strains from their sickest patients. Making life difficult for virulent microbes can actually guide the species' evolution, weeding out the most harmful variants. In the case of malaria, the trick is keeping mosquitoes away from people bedridden with virulent strains. "If you mosquito-proof the houses," says Ewald, "then only people walking around outside can spread the disease, and that will be a mild form."

Evolutionary theorists may be able to guess how specific microbes will evolve, but not the fate of the whole panoply of life. "You can't predict what organisms will look like millions of years from now," says Knoll. Chance events, small and large, make all the difference, as mutations arise at random and unpredictable mass extinctions set life on a new course.

One mass extinction is easy to foresee: the one already underway because of our logging and paving and polluting. Things don't look good for most large mammals—they can't compete with us for space and resources. The outlook is brighter for species that depend on humans, like farm animals and crop plants, as well as rats and cockroaches. But this mass extinction is different from the last, 65 million years ago. "The day after the meteorite hit," says Knoll, "the planet started to heal. The problem now doesn't go away. It gets bad and it stays bad as long as our evolutionary history continues."

God and Man

Which brings us to one final result of evolution, the odd, upright, and curiously self-obsessed ape in the mirror.

We've turned the tables on evolution, curing diseases and changing our environment to suit us, rather than the other way around. But don't think that frees us from further evolutionary changes. Incurable epidemics that strike the young are still a powerful selective force. A mutation that boosted resistance to HIV, for example, could spread quickly by allowing those who have it to survive and have children. "We continue to accumulate mutations," says Sarah Tishkoff, a geneticist at the University of Maryland. "But we're altering evolution." Assisted reproduction allows some people to beat natural selection, she notes, while birth control gives an evolutionary leg up to those who don't use it.

A quick survey of the human condition reveals any number of desirable improvements—surely evolution could take care of hernias and osteoporosis and the appendix, which serves no greater purpose than to become inflamed? But those annoyances usually don't keep the annoyed from passing on their genes. And with precious little geographic isolation—one of the main drivers of speciation—left in our global village, we'll probably have to wait until a space colony gets cut off for several thousand generations before a new human species evolves.

Of course, it's the idea that human beings themselves are products of evolution that provokes most of the attacks on evolution. Such rejections leave most scientists mystified. "The scientific narrative of the history of life is as exciting and imbued with mystery as any other telling of that story," says Knoll. The evidence against evolution amounts to little more than "'I can't imagine it,'" Ewald adds. "That's not evidence. That's just giving up."

Many researchers simply ignore the debates and press on with their work. But as evolution becomes an applied science, others say it's more urgent than ever to defend its place in the schools. "HIV is one of the world's most aggressively evolving organisms," says Palumbi. If it weren't for the virus's adaptability, which helps it foil the body's defenses and many drugs, "we would have kicked HIV in the teeth 15 years ago." But doctors don't learn about evolution in medical school, he says, leaving them about as well prepared to combat HIV as a flat-Earth astronomer would be to plan a moon shot.

"Somewhere in high school in this country is a student who's going to cure AIDS," Palumbi says. "That student is going to have to understand evolution."

When people discuss natural selection, they almost always discuss external circumstances that force organisms to adapt or die: predation, temperature, moisture, and food availability. A radical new idea is beginning to gain currency among some evolutionary biologists, however. They believe that an organism, by altering its own environment, can dramatically change the

direction or impact of natural selection. Rather than the environment acting upon it, the organism can also act upon its surroundings, affecting its own evolution and that of other organisms that share the same ecosystem. The authors of this selection call the new idea "niche construction." A good example of niche construction at work is provided by dairy farming. When people began to dairy farm, most humans could not fully digest cow's milk. Many people did not have the genes necessary to create the enzymes that break down lactose, a sugar found in milk. Yet, over time, increased dairy farming and milk consumption seem to have actually created natural selection pressure, resulting in the development of the enzyme that allows us to digest cow's milk more completely. —KH

"Life's Little Builders"
by Kevin Laland and John Odling-Smee
New Scientist, November 15, 2003

Think about evolution and you'll probably conjure up a picture of natural selection sculpting organisms over aeons of time to become adapted to specific environments. Hot climates select animals with heat-dispersing adaptations, such as large ears or the ability to pant. But no matter how much an animal flaps its ears or pants, it is not going to affect the local temperature to any significant extent. Environments shape living things: it rarely works the other way around. At least, that is the conventional view of evolution.

But how does this square with the seemingly innocent observation that the activities of all living creatures bring about changes in their environments? We are not just talking about birds constructing nests, spiders spinning webs and beavers engineering dams. There is much more to this process of "niche construction" than the creations of charismatic animals. Plants change levels of atmospheric gases, modify nutrient cycles, engage in chemical warfare, promote forest fires, create shade and alter wind speeds. Fungi decompose organic matter, weather rocks and extract minerals. Even bacteria and the simplest single-celled creatures leave the world in a different state from how they found it, through decomposition, photosynthesis, nutrient fixation or by initiating ecological processes that allow other organisms to colonise new environments. Surely these changes must influence evolution?

For several years now we have been grappling with this conundrum. Together with our colleague Marcus Feldman from Stanford University in California, we have been trying to assess the full extent of niche construction and its implications for evolutionary biology and ecology. Our studies have convinced us that niche construction should be recognised as a significant cause of evolution, on a par with natural selection. We are arguing for nothing less than a rethink of the evolutionary process itself. By accepting that organisms shape environments as surely as environments shape organisms, evolution is transformed from a linear to a cyclic process. This feedback allows successive generations of organisms to influence their own and each other's evolution.

If this feedback between organisms and their environments is so crucial to evolution, why hasn't it been recognised before? The answer is that niche construction is considered in certain limited situations, but rarely in terms that fully capture its evolutionary ramifications. Arguably the most influential description of the interaction between living things and the environments they inhabit comes from Richard Dawkins, in his book *The Extended Phenotype*. According to Dawkins, "an animal artefact . . . can be regarded as a phenotypic tool by which that gene could potentially lever itself into the next generation." He argues that genes build environmental states—the "extended phenotypes" of the title—to their own ends, reaching beyond the bodies of organisms to be expressed in the construction of webs, mounds and bowers.

Like most other evolutionary biologists, Dawkins views niche construction as a product of naturally selected genes, not a part of the evolutionary process itself. Put another way, the only relevant evolutionary feedback from extended phenotypes is to the genes that express them. So when beavers build dams, they ensure the propagation of "genes for" dam building, but that is all.

Yet by constructing their own niche, beavers radically alter their environment in many ways. With dams come calm, protective lakes, safe havens for their artificial island homes or lodges as well as for stores of food in the form of saplings saved for the winter. By cutting down trees, beavers alter the local hydrology, creating wetlands that may persist for centuries and influence plant and animal diversity. All this "engineering" is likely to modify natural selection not only for the genes associated with niche-constructing activities, but also for other genes expressed in quite different traits, such as beavers' life history, tails, teeth, foraging behaviour, susceptibility to predation and diseases—not to mention the evolutionary effect they have on other animals that share their altered environment.

You need look no further than the humble earthworm to see the power of niche construction. Across the globe, earthworms have dramatically changed the structure and chemistry of soil by burrowing, dragging plant material into the soil, mixing it up with inorganic material such as sand, and mulching the lot by ingesting and excreting it as worm casts. The scale of these earthworks is vast. What's more, because earthworm activities result in cumulative improvements in soil over long periods of time, it follows that today's earthworms inhabit environments that have been radically altered by their ancestors.

In other words, some extended phenotypes can be inherited. Through niche construction, organisms not only acquire genes from their ancestors but also an "ecological inheritance"—a legacy of natural selection pressures that have been modified by ancestors and that, in turn, shape subsequent generations. In the case of earthworms, some characters, such as the structure of their epidermis, or the amount of mucus they secrete and the strange physiology of their kidneys—as Scott Turner from the State University of New York in Syracuse describes in his book *The Extended Organism*—probably co-evolved with niche construction over many generations.

Ecological inheritance does not depend on the presence of biological replicators, but only on the persistence of physical changes made by ancestral organisms in the environments of their descendants. This kind of inheritance, which has been largely overlooked by evolutionary biologists, has more in common with the passing of property from generation to generation than that of genes. We believe it can be found throughout nature wherever generations of organisms progressively alter the environment in which their descendants live—not least in our own species, where children are born into a world elaborately created by the planet's virtuoso niche constructor. And ecological inheritance has important implications for understanding human evolution. For example, it challenges the idea that humans are adapted to an ancestral environment that existed from about 1.8 million years ago on the African savannah, an idea argued most vociferously by evolutionary psychologists.

Close inspection of the niche-constructing activities of countless organisms, from bacteria to humans, has convinced us that this is an important evolutionary process. But we are aware that we are not going to persuade others to abandon the conventional evolutionary perspective unless we can show that the feedback from niche construction is substantial. To that end, we have carried out mathematical analyses using population genetics models. They reveal that niche construction is far from inconsequential.

We found that niche construction forges new evolutionary pathways for species, sometimes allowing apparently damaging mutations to become incorporated into populations, at other times removing characters that seem well adapted, or creating new equilibria between alternative genetic forms. What's more, ecological inheritance can generate time lags in a population's response to selection. These manifest as curious "momentum effects" (where populations continue to evolve in the same direction after selection has stopped or reversed), "inertia effects" (where there is no noticeable evolutionary response to selection for several generations), and unpredictable or catastrophic responses to selection. In other words, niche construction can dramatically change the evolutionary dynamic.

Niche construction is not simply a product of prior natural selection of genetic traits, as most evolutionary biologists contend. It is a separate process that creates evolutionary pressures in its own right. This is particularly obvious when you look at genetic changes that have come about as a result of niche-constructing activities which are not themselves guaranteed by specific genes. The woodpecker finch of the Galapagos Islands, for example, uses a cactus spine to peck for insects under bark. It has no "grubbing genes" per se, but instead uses a more general and flexible adaptation— the ability to learn. Nonetheless, the birds' learned activities have apparently created selection pressures favouring a bill capable of wielding tools, rather than the long, pointed bill characteristic of woodpeckers.

Another example of a niche-constructing behaviour leading to genetic change is found in our own species. Around the world, the ability of adults to consume dairy products without becoming sick—lactose tolerance—reflects their ancestors' history of dairy farming. Recent genetic analysis reveals that dairy farming emerged before the spread of the genes that allow adults to digest lactose (the energy-rich sugar in milk), indicating that the practice of dairying almost certainly created the natural selection pressures that favoured these genes.

Incorporating such feedback loops into evolutionary models will certainly create some headaches, but the new perspective offers some major benefits. In particular, it has the potential to unify evolution and ecology in a way that has not been possible until now.

At first sight, ecology appears thoroughly evolutionary. But take a closer look and you find that not all ecologists use evolutionary methods. Ecosystem ecologists paid a high price for accommodating Darwinism, namely the division of their field into two approaches: "population-community ecology," which takes an evolutionary perspective, and "process-functional ecology," which does not. Superficially, these two sub-fields appear to be separated by little more than their choice of subject matter, but in practice they have proved remarkably difficult to integrate.

Typically, process-functional ecologists ask questions about the composition of ecosystems, their scale and their boundaries, their structural and functional design, and their regulation. One of their principal goals is to understand how energy and matter flow through both living and nonliving parts of an ecosystem. So they often grapple with complete biogeochemical cycles such as the carbon or nitrogen cycle. In contrast, population-community ecologists concentrate primarily on organisms. For them, living creatures are the ecosystem, and the nonliving components (soil, water and so on) are largely viewed as backdrops to the tapestry of life.

The key sticking point is that nonliving components do not evolve. Take the carbon cycle. Carbon typically enters a living community when atmospheric CO_2 is fixed by plants and bacteria in photosynthesis. Later it becomes available for consumption by herbivores as cellulose and sugar, and subsequently by carnivores, as fat and protein, before being released back into the environment through respiration, decay and other processes. In the soil, it may be taken up again by organisms or washed away by rain.

Living, evolving organisms obviously play a huge role in the carbon cycle, but the carbon in the atmosphere, soils, rivers and oceans is effectively out of bounds for evolutionary theory. As a result, ecologists are left with a tough choice. They can pretend that evolution has stopped and incorporate the nonliving components, allowing them to study chemical cycles such as the carbon cycle, but only in terms of flows of energy and matter. Or they can incorporate evolution, but at the cost of editing out the physical environment. This division makes it difficult to build a complete picture of some of the central players in ecosystems. But the niche construction perspective offers a way out of this impasse. By emphasising the role of organisms in modifying and controlling environmental resources, it provides evolutionary methods that apply to nonliving resources too.

While most ecologists do not yet think organisms can orchestrate ecosystems, a growing number are seeing the benefit of incorporating these ideas into their thinking. They include Clive Jones of the Institute of Ecosystem Studies in Millbrook, New York, and his colleagues John Lawton from the Centre for Population Biology at Silwood Park, UK, and Moshe Shachak from Ben-Gurion University at Sede Boqer, Israel. They have been studying "ecosystem engineering" in a wide variety of species, including three species of snail of the genus Euchondrus, which eat lichens that grow under the surface of rocks in the Negev desert in Israel. One consequence of this unusual form of herbivory is that the snails play a major role in eroding rock.

It's not that these snails consume large amounts of lichens—they don't—but rather that they have to ingest rock to get at the lichens underneath. They later excrete this as faeces, which becomes soil. The researchers estimated that the annual rate of biological weathering of these rocks by snails is approximately 1 tonne per hectare, which is sufficient to affect the whole desert ecosystem. By converting rock to soil at this rate, the snails are major agents in both soil formation and nitrogen cycling, and critical to the establishment of higher plant communities.

Studies like this show that a focus on niche construction provides ecologists with fresh tools for linking species to ecosystems. The potential of this approach is considerable. For instance, it might allow ecologists to predict which species will invade a community and what their impact will be, depending on the species' ability to tolerate the effects of niche construction by other populations and the nature of their own engineering effects. It also suggests a host of new empirical methods, such as tracing the niche construction of populations round entire ecosystems, and identifying particular modifications of the environment associated with specific genes.

Niche construction may also shed light on some of ecology's biggest questions. For instance, nature seems so harmonious and coordinated that some have wondered whether ecosystems are super-organisms. In his Gaia hypothesis, James Lovelock went so far as to use the metaphor of a living entity with powers of self-regulation to describe Earth. But understanding niche construction allows you to see ecosystems not as mysterious super-organisms, but rather as super-constructions created by the collective activities of their constituent organisms. The impacts of niche construction thread entire ecosystems, binding them together—which explains their impressive structural and functional integration and underlies the illusion that they are alive. Yet, since not all niche construction imposes order, it also explains why other ecosystems are not functionally integrated but are the messy, uncoordinated outcomes of several species pulling in different directions.

Nowhere is this more apparent than in some man-made environments. Understanding the impact of our own activities on ecosystems and on evolution could give us new insights into the legacy we are creating. It might even help us find ways to reduce the damaging consequences of our actions. For example, conservation efforts might be more effective if they ensured the survival of the key niche constructors within any ecosystem. Researchers studying niche construction and ecosystem engineering are devising new tools for identifying these.

But their future work may provide an even more radical approach to conservation because, in some cases, the best way to preserve an ecosystem may be to preserve the niche-constructing effects of particular animals or plants in it, rather than the species themselves. So niche construction could offer a new kind of medicine for sick ecosystems.

Reprinted with permission from *New Scientist*.

Starting with Charles Darwin, evolutionary biologists have long theorized that natural selection was all about competition. Earth cannot sustain all the life that is upon it, so organisms must compete for survival. Generally, the stronger and more adaptable will do better than those who are weaker and less able to adapt to changing conditions. This is natural selection at work—only the strong survive. The natural

world would seem to be a cold and hostile place, driven strictly by selfish, every-organism-for-itself action. But what role does cooperation among organisms play in nature? Corals rely on symbiotic algae, bats feed weak neighbors, and ants give up reproduction to work tirelessly for their egg-laying queen. Cooperation among organisms is, in fact, quite common. Yet author James Randerson argues that nearly everywhere you look there is an underlying selfish reason for such camaraderie. Some individuals help others because they will be helped themselves in the future and because the cost of helping is less than its beneficial effects. Ants help their nest mates, many argue, simply because they are so closely related to them. If the goal of all organisms is to pass on their genetic material, an ant that helps its closely related sister survive long enough to reproduce is, in a sense, ensuring the survival of its own genetic material. —KH

"Together We Are Stronger"
by James Randerson
New Scientist, **March 15, 2003**

In nature's rough and tumble, compassion is for wimps. The struggle to survive means being fastest to the kill, beating off rivals for a mate, and dealing with parasites and infections better than the rest. Mother Nature does not hand out prizes for second place . . .

But where does that leave cooperation? If it's "every ant for herself" how come worker ants forgo their own chances of breeding to take on dangerous work in the service of the queen, and why do vampire bats sometimes regurgitate food for a neighbour who isn't even related? Come to that, if it weren't for cooperation and altruism, there'd be no human civilisation. Although conflict may grab the headlines, when you look more closely it's cooperation that makes the world go round. But biologists are finding that among non-human creatures, at least, being nice is rooted in selfishness.

Life's amazing ability to propagate itself means there will never be enough resources to go round. The humble bacterium *Escherichia coli*, for example, can divide every 20 minutes in optimum conditions. Starting from a single cell and keeping that up for just a day would result in so many bacteria that, if laid end to end, they would stretch seven thousand billion kilometres, or more than a thousand times the distance between Pluto and the Sun. In the wild, fortunately—unlike in the lab—"optimum conditions" are nowhere to be found. Organisms have to compete for what's available.

According to Darwin, it is competition for resources that keeps populations in check. Only those best suited to their environment survive to spawn the next generation. In his book *On the Origin of Species* he coined the term natural selection and compared it to selective breeding by humans. Over hundreds of years, pigeon fanciers and dog breeders have selected animals with desirable attributes and bred from them. Slowly but surely, the pigeon's ruff or the greyhound's speed became exaggerated, until the resulting beast is all but unrecognisable next to its rock dove or wolf ancestor. Selection, be it artificial or natural, works because individuals display a range of characteristics that are heritable—they can be passed on to future generations.

Darwin struggled to understand the mechanisms of heredity, because he knew nothing of genes or genetics. But we're now aware that different individuals in a population possess different alleles—alternative versions of a gene at a particular location in the genome. By coding for slightly different variants of the same proteins, these alleles can produce different physical characteristics, such as darker-coloured fur that blends in better with the surroundings. Those lucky enough to have the dark-fur allele are less likely to be seen and eaten by predators—they are better adapted to their environment—and are more likely to pass on their genes. Over several generations, the dark-fur allele may spread through the entire population. Occasionally, random mutations will create completely new alleles that give individuals the edge in a particular environment. These are the raw material of evolution, and conflict between those with different alleles is its driving force.

So at first sight, the popularity of cooperation is something of a mystery. Even different species do it. Symbiotic relationships are everywhere. Coral polyps cannot survive without the photosynthetic algae that live in their tissues. Trees exchange nutrients with the fungi plugged into their roots. Termites owe their ability to digest wood to the symbiotic microbes living in their gut. And each lichen "species" is in fact a different symbiotic relationship between a fungus and a green alga or cyanobacterium.

Cooperation within species is just as popular. In East Africa, naked mole rats live in underground colonies of about 80 individuals, but only one pair breeds. The rest selflessly feed the young and defend the nest. Also in East Africa, colonies of pied kingfishers often include helpers who don't breed but spend their time catching fish for the breeding pair—to whom they may be only distantly related. Cooperation is everywhere we look, but how does working for others help an organism to pass on its own genes?

One suggestion—now discredited—was that selection acts not on individuals but on groups of organisms. Let's say we have two populations of great tits [small, plump, usually long-tailed birds], one selfless and the other selfish. In the selfish group each female lays eight eggs—the number that will ensure that as many of her own offspring as possible will survive. But what's good for her isn't good for the population as a whole because these extra mouths will put a heavy strain on the food supply. So parents have to compete to harvest enough to feed their own broods. Meanwhile in the cooperative group, mothers lay just enough eggs (three, say) to keep the population at a stable level without threatening the food supply. Biologists who argued in favour of group selection claimed that the selfish population would starve to death by scoffing all the food, while the more selfless, "civilised" birds—and their genes—prospered.

This looks fine on paper, but cheating is rife in nature. In the cooperative group, a few birds may guzzle the plentiful food but cheat on their fellows by raising massive broods. Behaviour like this could arise from a mutation or perhaps if a female defects from the selfish group. While food is still plentiful, sneaky alleles like these will spread rapidly. So although group selection makes sense in theory as an explanation for cooperation, it doesn't work too well in practice. Indeed, studies on real great tits have found no evidence that females restrict their clutch sizes to protect the food supply for the good of the population or the species. Instead, each lays enough eggs to maximise the number of surviving chicks she will rear in her lifetime.

So how did cooperation ever get going? It turns out there are ways cooperation can evolve even among selfish individuals and selfish genes. The most obvious way is through mutual benefit. If a partnership is good for both parties, then even the selfish will enter into it. There are plenty of examples of mutualism in nature. Trees and the fungi living on their roots both gain by their association. The fungus takes advantage of carbohydrates manufactured in the leaves, and the tree benefits because the fungus provides minerals that are difficult to extract from the soil. It's a give-and-take relationship.

Mutualism can operate within species as well. As a defence against predators, prey animals such as zebra and wildebeest opt for safety in numbers. Herds form for purely selfish reasons because, although they make the prey more visible, being part of a crowd lowers each individual's risk of being singled out for attack. Group membership also allows you to take advantage of the vigilance provided by many pairs of ears, eyes and nostrils.

Honour Among Vampires

Cooperation doesn't have to bring immediate benefits. In a reciprocal relationship, an individual gives help in the expectation that at some time in the future it will receive help in return. This arrangement is much harder to get off the ground than mutualism because of the scope for cheats to receive help but never reciprocate. But there are examples in nature. In Costa Rica, vampire bats sometimes regurgitate part of their blood meal for colony mates who have had an unsuccessful night's feeding. Interestingly, this only happens between related individuals or bats that frequently hang from neighbouring perches. And in lab experiments where researchers could control which bats fed and which did not, individuals who had received food on other occasions were more likely to feed their benefactor at a later date. The arrangement is truly reciprocal.

A crucial feature of the interaction is that feeding is more beneficial to the recipient than it is costly to the donor. For a well-fed bat, giving up 5 percent of a blood meal might take it a couple of hours closer to starvation. But for a hungry bat, that donated meal could take it 15 or 20 hours further away from death. Individuals may be prepared to pay a small cost for the prospect of much greater—albeit uncertain—future rewards.

The phrase "blood is thicker than water" is certainly true for vampire bats: they're more likely to give up some of their meal to family members. It also neatly sums up the genetic mechanism behind the most mind-blowing products of cooperation, the social insects. Worldwide there are 12,000 or so social insect species, roughly equivalent to the number of bird and mammal species put together. In the hymenoptera alone (the group that includes ants, bees and wasps) social living is thought to have evolved independently at least 11 times.

A common feature of species that live in colonies is that they are eusocial, meaning sterile workers help their parents. So a worker ant, bee or wasp forgoes her own chances of reproduction in order to rear her sisters. This is difficult to explain if we assume selection acts on individuals. But suppose it acts at the level of their genes. Organisms are merely vehicles that genes use to hitch a ride into the next generation. The route can be direct, through reproduction, or indirect, by helping others who have a copy of the same gene to breed. It doesn't matter. (Biologists talk of direct fitness and indirect fitness to distinguish the two. The sum of the two is called inclusive fitness.)

So if a female has a particular allele and she helps out with the rearing of her sisters, maximising the productivity of the egg-laying machine that is the queen, the allele will still get passed on because the chances are her sisters and the queen have it too. It's called kin selection.

In 1963, the British geneticist William Hamilton reduced the idea of kin selection to a mathematical equation that predicts whether a particular altruistic behaviour will evolve. Hamilton's rule says one organism should only help another if B/C is greater than 1/r, where B is the benefit to the recipient in terms of more offspring, C is the cost to the helper in terms of fewer offspring, and r is the proportion of genes they share, known as their coefficient of relatedness.

One strong prediction of the rule is that the more closely related the recipient is to the donor, the more often it pays to help. For example, the coefficient of relatedness between you and your mother is exactly 0.5. You have half of your genes in common. So if helping her is to work in your favour, B/C has to be greater than two—the benefit to your mum has to be at least twice the cost to you. On the other hand, the coefficient of relatedness between you and your cousin is only 0.125 (on average you share an eighth of your genes). So helping a cousin only pays off if the benefit to them is eight times as great as the cost to you. The chances are you won't bother.

The Belding's ground squirrel from the far western US illustrates this preference for helping close kin. The rodents live in groups and give alarm calls to warn others if a predator such as a coyote is near. Sounding an alarm is probably risky because it draws the predator's attention to the caller. And, just as the theory of kin selection predicts, an individual is more likely to take this risk if there are close relatives nearby.

The hymenoptera use a genetic system called haplodiploidy that might predispose them to social living.

Rather than both parents contributing an equal number of genes to the offspring, as humans do, female bees can produce viable eggs without a male. If the egg is not fertilised it develops into a male and is haploid (has one copy of each chromosome), but if it is fertilised it becomes a female and is diploid (has two copies of each). The upshot of this is that females are more closely related to their sisters than they would be to their own daughters. Why? Imagine a particular pair of chromosomes in a female bee. One came from her mother, one from her father. Father is haploid, so all her sisters will have at least one chromosome from this pair in common: they share at least half the genes. But mother is diploid, so half our bee's sisters will have got the same chromosome as her and half will have got the other. On average, they have three-quarters of all their genes in common: they are more closely related than they would be to their own daughters. No wonder they evolved into sterile helpers.

Haplodiploidy can't be the whole story, though, because there are social species of aphid, termite and even spider, and none of them uses the haplodiploid system. But there's another, perhaps even bigger advantage of social living: it allows division of labour. Freed from carrying out every kind of chore, an individual can specialise. This might mean becoming more efficient at a task through practice, or simply not wasting time and energy switching between different jobs. In honeybees, for example, workers take on different roles as they age. Those under 2 days old clean cells, from 2 to 11 days they care for the queen and brood, aged 11 to 20 days they process food arriving at the nest, and after 20 days they go out foraging.

No matter how cooperation evolves, however, the biggest threat to it is cheating: individuals reaping the benefits without contributing. The prisoner's dilemma is a thought experiment from a branch of mathematics called game theory illustrating why it's so difficult to avoid freeloaders. Imagine two crooks called Charlie and Ronnie who are picked up by the police on the way home from a bank job. The bumbling cops have some evidence, but not enough to convict them. They know full well that Charlie and Ronnie are guilty, if only they can sweat it out of them.

In separate cells, the police give each a choice: either they can stay quiet (cooperate) or squeal on their pal and get a lighter sentence (defect). Game theory assigns scores to the different outcomes, showing how each prisoner would benefit. If Charlie and Ronnie both stay buttoned up, they will be put away for only a couple of months based on the meagre evidence the police already have (30 points). But if Charlie keeps quiet and is grassed up by Ronnie he will end up with a stiff jail term (10 points), while Ronnie gets off scotfree (40 points). On the other hand, if both prisoners do the dirty on each other, they receive a relatively long stretch behind bars (20 points) but less than if they had taken the full rap.

Suppose Charlie trusts Ronnie to keep shtum [quiet] : what should he do? If he keeps his mouth shut too he gets 30 points, but if he defects he gets a stonking [whopping] 40. So defecting is the best option. But suppose Charlie thinks Ronnie will defect. If Charlie keeps quiet he'll get a measly 10, so even the prospect of a longish spell in the slammer for defecting (and a modest 20) looks worthwhile. So, paradoxically, defecting is always the best option for both players, even though they'd do better if they cooperated. So much for the old adage that there's honour among thieves.

How did humans and other social animals escape the prisoner's dilemma? Perhaps the game doesn't always reflect real life. A more realistic situation would be one in which participants play each other more than once, reacting to how the other behaved in previous games. This raises the possibility of more complex strategies that involve a combination of cooperating and defecting. In 1980, Robert Axelrod, a political scientist at the University of Michigan, set up a round-robin tournament between 64 different strategies submitted by academics and enthusiasts from around the world. Each strategy, in the form of a computer program, competed against the others and itself.

The strategy that amassed the most points was a simple one called "Tit for Tat." A TFT player cooperates on the first move, but subsequently copies whatever its opponent did in the previous round. So TFT is a strategy based on reciprocity that punishes a defection by the opponent, but is also quick to forgive.

Another way to bolster cooperation is to set up a social contract. Individuals entering into the contract agree to punish defectors. The cost of punishing is −5 while the cost of being punished is −50. In this case, a "cooperate and punish" strategy scores 25 (30−5), but a "defect and be punished" strategy scores a pitiful −10 (40−50).

Such an intricate mechanism might seem a little far-fetched, but animal cooperatives often have inbuilt ways to punish cheats. In bee colonies, for example, workers retain the ability to lay male, unfertilised eggs. This is in their own genetic interests but not those of their sisters, because in the process the laying workers neglect their colony duties. Sure enough, if other workers detect such eggs they destroy them.

It is highly evolved behaviours like this that have made social insects so successful. Collectives such as bee and ant hives have even been described as super-organisms. But their evolution is just the latest in a long line of transitions from lower to higher levels of organisation. For example, primitive genes clubbed together to form genomes and single cells banded together to become multicellular organisms. At every stage the same principles apply. Cooperation brings rich pickings by allowing division of labour and mutual benefit, but cheats who take the spoils without contributing must somehow be kept to a minimum or the venture fails.

One such cooperative venture led to the evolution of eukaryotes (cells with nuclei) from more primitive cells (prokaryotes). The Endosymbiotic Theory argues that the organelles of eukaryotic cells are the descendants of prokaryotes that were engulfed by larger prokaryotic cells around 2.1 billion years ago (see "Cellular factories," *Inside Science*, No. 95).

The next cooperative step came when single-celled organisms got together to form primitive multicellular organisms. The bizarre creatures known as slime moulds (*Dictyostelium discoideum*) provide an extraordinary action replay of what might have happened. Single-celled slime moulds spend most of their time scavenging food in moist soil. But if the food supply runs out, between 10,000 and 50,000 individual cells come together to form a fruiting body. This looks much like the stamen of a flower, with a bundle of spores on top of a rigid stalk. It also serves the same function, dispersing the spores by releasing them into the wind.

But even in slime mould society there are cheats, because although cells that become spores get to spread their genes far and wide, stalk cells are doomed. Kin selection helps because the spores and stalk cells are related, so the sacrifice by the stalk cells benefits genes they have in common with the spores. However, fruiting bodies often contain cells from two different, less closely related groups, and sometimes one of the groups cheats by contributing more than its fair share of spores, leaving the other group to build most of the stalk.

There can be little doubt: selfish genes are behind both cheating and cooperation. Despite the existence of so much teamwork in the natural world, Darwin's vision of nature red in tooth and claw still holds true, because if you dig deep enough, cooperation is always underpinned by genes looking after number one. But watch out: in nearly every successful team there are free-loaders who are happy to sit back and reap the rewards of everyone else's hard work.

Reprinted with permission from *New Scientist*.

Evolution, Adaptation, and Extinction

2

Gary Larson, arguably the most beloved cartoonist among biologists, captured the essence of science in thousands of drawings for his syndicated comic strip The Far Side. In one famous and often reproduced panel, two huge dinosaurs loom over a strange, furry creature at their feet. One dinosaur points and laughs at the mammal's strangeness, while the other looks up, beholding something new—snow—in what had previously been a largely tropical world. Larson's point is that mammals may have seemed bizarre during the time of the great lizards, but these new, furry, warm-blooded creatures were far better equipped to cope with and adapt to the impending climate change. Larson and many biologists may have gotten it wrong, however. As Richard A. Kerr points out in this article, recent paleontological studies have called into question the central importance of climate change to mammal evolution and the rapidity with which climate change can spark specieswide adaptation or extinction. —KH

"New Mammal Data Challenge Evolutionary Pulse Theory"
by Richard A. Kerr
Science, July 26, 1996

Paleontologists anxious to make sense of the rise and fall of species in the fossil record have long invoked climate change as a prime mover in evolution, a force that triggers the evolution of new species while condemning others to extinction. But although there are plenty of rough correlations between climate change and evolution, proving a causal link has been difficult, given the imperfect preservation of the geologic record.

In the 1980s, however, paleontologist Elisabeth Vrba of Yale University documented a striking coincidence in the African geologic record about 2.6 million years ago, when a major climatic step toward the ice-age world occurred just as African antelopes underwent a burst of evolution and extinction. Adding popular appeal to the work, the human family tree branched out at about the same time, giving rise to the lineage that eventually led to *Homo sapiens*. Vrba proposed that a single climate-driven "turnover pulse" involving antelopes, hominids, and other animals had in a geologic moment turned evolution in a fateful new direction.

The idea attracted much attention, but few paleontologists managed to test it. Now new data reported at the North American Paleontological Convention (NAPC) in Washington, D.C., last month raise doubts about the theory. One of the richest, best dated African fossil records—which includes some of the same species

Vrba studied—shows no sign of a turnover pulse. Rather, it shows "a more sustained shift" over a million years or more from woodland species toward grassland species, says Anna K. Behrensmeyer of the Smithsonian Institution's National Museum of Natural History, who led the study. "There was global change," she says, "but its effect on the fauna was not punctuated."

This and other new work could provide new ammunition to those who see a limited role for climate change in evolution. "I'm a real skeptic" about the effects of climate change, says mammal paleontologist Richard Stucky of the Denver Museum of Natural History. "When you look at the whole range of species, very seldom is there a climate event that changes the course of mammalian evolution." But even as new data come in, it's clear that the subject of how changing climate affects mammalian evolution continues to spark a range of opinions, with Stucky's minimal role at one extreme, Vrba's turnover pulse at another, and Behrensmeyer's prolonged shift somewhere in between.

Vrba wasn't at the meeting to defend the turnover pulse idea—she's on sabbatical in South Africa. (She also could not be reached for this article, despite repeated attempts to locate her through colleagues in the United States and Africa.) But her latest data were published late last year in two conference proceedings charters. She compiled her own and published records of the first and last appearances of 147 species of African antelopes, most from eastern and southern Africa, during the past 7 million years. That analysis showed that from 3 million to 2 million years ago, the total number of species doubled, and 90 % of all species recorded in that interval either first appeared or went extinct during that time. Furthermore, almost all of this considerable turnover was concentrated between 2.7 million and 2.5 million years ago. Meanwhile, although the exact timing is in dispute, the genus *Homo* also appeared between 3 million and 2 million years ago, possibly right about 2.5 million years ago.

Climatic data are consistent with Vrba's theory too. After about 3 million years ago, Earth was gradually cooling, as the climate system headed toward glaciation in the Northern Hemisphere. But Africa didn't slide smoothly toward the ice ages—it jumped, according to Peter deMenocal of Columbia University's Lamont-Doherty Earth Observatory (*Science*, 14 January 1994, p. 173). By analyzing climate indicators in marine muds off the African coasts, he showed that between 2.8 million and 2.6 million years ago, subtropical Africa's climate abruptly shifted from one mode of operation to another, switching from a 20,000-year beat controlled by Earth's wobbling on its rotation axis to a more intense, 40,000-year beat driven by the changing tilt of the axis. This new regime left tropical Africa oscillating between a warmer, wetter climate and a cooler, drier one.

Vrba suggests that the longer, cooler episodes drove antelope evolution by means of a classic mechanism— breaking up the antelope's preferred woodland habitat into isolated ecological islands scattered among grass-lands. The small woodland populations then spawned new species better adapted to the grasslands. Her hypothesis predicts that other species, including hominids, would respond the same way. As might be expected, such a sweeping generalization drew strong reactions. Those who didn't see pulses in their data were doubtful, while those whose world view includes abrupt evolutionary steps were enthusiastic. "The idea is wonderful," says Niles Eldredge of the American Museum of Natural History in New York City, co-creator of the theory of punctuated equilibrium.

But testing Vrba's idea requires an unusually rich and well-dated fossil record. One such record is a new computerized database developed under the Evolution of Terrestrial Ecosystems program run by the National Museum of Natural History. This includes the first and last appearances of 510 mammal taxa ranging from antelopes to baboons for the past 6 million years. For their test, the group focused on the fossiliferous and well-studied Lake Turkana region of East Africa, which has yielded a variety of animals, including hominids. What's more, the Turkana fossils are the best dated in Africa for the period from 1 million to 4 million years ago, thanks to repeated volcanic eruptions that blanketed the region with radiometrically datable ash layers.

When the Smithsonian team plotted the pace of evolution in the Turkana fauna about 2.5 million years ago, the turnover pulse theory "just didn't seem to hold up," says Behrensmeyer. "Clearly, there was a shift going on, but I think we can show the event was occurring over at least a million years and doesn't qualify as a pulse." Instead of a 90% turnover in a few hundred thousand years, the team found a 50 % to 60 % turnover spread between 3 million and 2 million years ago. Diversity during the period rose 30 % rather than doubling, as Vrba reported for the antelopes. Even for the 53 species common to both studies, there is little sign of a Turkana pulse, says Behrensmeyer.

Slowing the pace of the shift toward grassland-adapted animals and starting it earlier blurs Vrba's link between evolutionary change and Africa's jump to a new climate mode. Instead, the Turkana data suggest that the fauna was steadily nudged toward grassland-adapted species by a global cooling and related African drying. "There isn't a pulse," says paleontologist David Pilbeam of Harvard University, who has seen the Smithsonian data. "I had considered that maybe around 2.5 million years ago there was sufficient environmental change that you would get a turnover pulse, but the evidence would now suggest that you didn't."

Exactly why Vrba's record for African antelopes is punctuated and the Turkana record isn't remains unclear. One possibility is that variations in fossil abundance through time skewed Vrba's data, creating a false peak. Another is that the Turkana rift valley—which held a river bounded by woodland at this time—was buffered from the dramatic climatic shifts, suggests paleontologist Steven Stanley of Johns Hopkins University. Testing whether the Turkana region was typical of Africa isn't yet practicable, says Pilbeam, noting that only in the Turkana basin is the African mammalian record detailed enough to offer a more or less complete documentation of the changing fauna. "If you really want to know what happened in Africa over the past 2 to 3 million years, you need many such [records]," he says. "The quality of record that we would need [to test the turnover pulse hypothesis] is way beyond what we currently have, and it may indeed be beyond what we are ever likely to have."

Detailed comparisons of methodology may eventually sort out why these African studies differ, but they are not likely to settle the broader question of how climate influences mammalian evolution. On that the record is mixed. In addition to Vrba's pulse and Behrensmeyer's slow drift, there are also reports of no mammal response at all to abrupt climate change. At the NAPC meeting, Donald Prothero of Occidental College in Los Angeles argued that two major cooling events 37 million and 33 million years ago failed to affect North American mammals, although these cold spells apparently triggered extinctions in the sea and among terrestrial nonmammals. "The mammal response is negligible," Prothero says. "There is no turnover pulse, at least in North America."

Yet previous studies have shown that climate can have at least an indirect effect on mammal evolution. For example, 33 million years ago, when North American mammals were blithely ignoring climate change, European mammals were suffering through "La Grande Coupure," or the great break. It was a brief but momentous evolutionary event in which up to 60% of European mammals went extinct, to be replaced by more modern forms (*Science*, 18 September 1992, p. 1622). But researchers think climate's role was indirect: A burst of glaciation created a land bridge to Asia, and the European mammals lost out to Asian invaders.

The dearth of evidence that climate change has forced mammalian extinction and speciation has Prothero and others questioning traditional assumptions. "We've oversold the idea that animals, especially land mammals, are responsive to environmental change," he says. "Animals seem to be remarkably resistant to a lot more change than we thought." All of which leaves open the question of why our favorite mammals, our ancestors, emerged in Africa as Earth was entering its ice age.

Reprinted with permission from Kerr, Richard A., "New Mammal Data Challenge Evolutionary Pulse Theory," SCIENCE 273:431 (1996). © 1996 AAAS.

Many biologists divide evolution into micro- and macroevolution. Microevolution refers to the accumulation of relatively small genetic changes and variations that occur within populations over time, while macroevolution is concerned with the large and complex transformations of a species that are often recorded in fossils. The following article addresses the final end point of macroevolutionary development—extinction. The reasons behind the extinction of North American mammoths (and others of the continent's largest animals, including mastodons, saber-toothed cats, and ground sloths) following the end of the last ice age is one of evolution's

enduring mysteries. Studying macroevolution is a bit like playing detective, and this particular "crime" remains unsolved. The leading suspects are known to us—our ancestors, who are accused of overhunting the large animals into extinction. As this article points out, however, more and more scientists are saying that not enough evidence exists to support this old theory and that the case might be far more complicated than it once appeared. Some combination of environmental stress, climate change, and human influence may have led to the disappearance of the continent's great beasts. Nevertheless, the sobering truth remains that humans can play a major role in evolution, including our uncanny ability to drive animals to extinction. We may not be guilty of the mammoths' ultimate demise, but we have plenty of other creatures' blood on our hands. —KH

"Scientists Question Whether Humans Caused Extinction of Mammoths"
by Alexandra Witze
Dallas Morning News, September 25, 2003

Call it North America's most mysterious mass killing. After millions of deaths, and with a chief suspect in custody, the case remains surprisingly circumstantial.

The defendant is humanity. At the end of the last ice age, most of North America's biggest animals disappeared. Mammoths, mastodons, saber-toothed cats and ground sloths all bit it—right after people first showed up by crossing a land bridge from Asia.

In a court of law, such evidence might be enough to convict humans of multiple 13,000-year-old murders. But a Dallas archaeologist, who happens to be a leading expert on the earliest Americans, thinks the case should be declared a mistrial.

The idea that spear-wielding humans hunted North America's mammoths and other giant animals to extinction has practically no archaeological support, says David Meltzer of Southern Methodist University. In recent months, he and Donald Grayson, of the University of Washington, have launched a campaign to declare humans not guilty of the mass slaughter.

"The evidence at hand simply doesn't support it," Meltzer says.

But that's not to say humans are entirely innocent. They may have unwittingly conspired with environmental factors, such as climate change, to wipe out the great animals. Without enough concrete clues, the crime remains unsolved.

During the last ice age, North America was home to big creatures that have since vanished. Many scientists think that humans, who first entered the continent at least 13,500 years ago, drove these animals to extinction through too much hunting. Others argue that a sudden cold snap that occurred around the same time may instead be to blame.

At the end of the Pleistocene epoch, 35 genuses of animals went extinct. A new study shows that evidence of human hunting exists for only two, mammoths and mastodons. No slaughtered bones remain of the saber-toothed cat Smilodon, the giant ground sloth Megatherium, or creatures such as cave bears, camels and the armadillo-like glyptodonts.

As in any trial, testimony appears conflicting. Other expert witnesses aren't exactly lining up behind Grayson and Meltzer. "I think they're way out on an anthropological limb, and they're sawing it off behind them," said mammoth expert Larry Agenbroad, of Northern Arizona University, in one of the kinder comments made about their work.

Meanwhile, two other archaeologists have written a detailed rebuttal that will appear in the *Journal of Archaeological Science*, the same journal that published Grayson and Meltzer's paper, "A requiem for North American overkill."

"I'm no lawyer, but circumstantial evidence does lead to conviction," says one of those authors, archaeologist Stuart Fiedel of the Louis Berger Group in Washington, D.C. "We do have a weapon here, and a pattern of behavior."

Few scientists working in the field claim to have all the answers. Something dramatic happened on this continent near the end of the Pleistocene epoch, 13,000 years ago. But whether it was due to slaughter by humans, climate change, a combination of the two, or something else—the jury remains out.

For a while, prosecutors seemed to be winning with their charges that humans were the killers. Ecologist

Paul Martin introduced the idea in the 1960s, and it quickly caught on among biologists for its simple explanation of a dramatic event.

"We've got some terrible kind of accident happening . . . right under our nose, and not enough attention has been paid to it," says Martin, a professor emeritus at the University of Arizona.

Overkill—the notion that excessive hunting by humans drove some big animals, or "megafauna," to extinction—seemed a straightforward explanation for their disappearance in North America and elsewhere. Humans showed up; animals went dead. It seemed tailor-made for the Discovery Channel.

"You've got big beefy hairy-chested blokes clumping across the prairies and whacking off megafauna with their big pointy spears," says Australian paleontologist Stephen Wroe. "You've got blood, you've got violence. It's Arnold Schwarzenegger does the late Pleistocene."

Most scientists accept the notion of overkill on islands because there are many clearly documented examples. Dodos went extinct on Mauritius soon after humans and accompanying animals showed up. Another group of big, flightless birds—called moas— was snuffed out on New Zealand.

But on islands as big as Australia, or continents like North America, the picture muddies.

Many paleontologists have attributed the deaths of Australia's megafauna to humans, who showed up there between 40,000 and 60,000 years ago. But there isn't a single confirmed "kill site"—evidence of deliberately slaughtered animals—from that time in the country, says Wroe, of the University of Sydney.

By comparison, archaeologists have identified many possible kill sites in North America. But Grayson and Meltzer dismantle much of that evidence in two recent papers.

The scientists used an electronic database to identify places with both artifacts of the first Americans and evidence of slaughtered megafauna.

Of the original 76 candidate sites, Grayson and Meltzer found only 14 that offered convincing evidence of hunting, they wrote in another publication, the *Journal of World Prehistory*.

Twelve of the sites contained mammoth bones, and two had mastodon. There's no evidence for kill sites for the other 33 genuses of large animals that also went extinct, including saber-toothed cats, armadillo-like glyptodonts, and ground sloths.

Overkill may have taken place, the archaeologists say, but there is slim evidence to support it.

Martin, overkill's spiritual father, has fought this challenge for years. The killing spree, he explains, would have happened so quickly—in a virtual "blitzkrieg" of several hundred years—the odds of finding archaeological evidence of it would be greatly reduced.

Another counterargument comes from Gary Haynes, an archaeologist at the University of Nevada in Reno and co-author of the *Journal of Archaeological Science* rebuttal. Fourteen kill sites, he says, is actually an extraordinarily high number.

Haynes has spent decades looking for dead elephants in Africa, documenting how often skeletons of slaughtered animals become preserved as fossils. The answer: not often.

"Africa has been occupied for a couple million years and people have been killing elephants over that time, but there are only six kill sites of elephants," Haynes says. For any sites at all to exist in North America, he argues, there must have been a lot of killing going on.

For his part, Meltzer doesn't dispute that early Americans hunted big animals. The question, to him, is whether the hunting was intensive enough to wipe out the megafauna forever. After all, a good number of big animal species—including bison, deer, elk and moose—made it through the end of the Pleistocene just fine.

"Human predation, despite being intensive and wasteful, does not necessarily lead to extinction on a continental scale," he says.

Other new lines of investigation may help scientists pinpoint the extinction cause.

One promising field is the study of ancient DNA. At a recent scientific meeting in Reno, Nev., University of Oxford biologist Alan Cooper described how fragments of DNA, preserved in bone or even in sediment, could reveal much about past animals' lives.

His work, for instance, has illuminated what moas were like on New Zealand before humans finished them off. And he's even studied ancient DNA from Siberia, particularly the area that was once connected to North America by the land bridge crossed by the first Americans.

This spring in *Science*, Cooper's team published dates for DNA remains of bison, horses and mammoths from Siberia. Such studies could reveal how populations of different animals changed over time and across geographic areas. It might even be possible, Meltzer says, to see whether some of those 35 genuses of big animals may have gone extinct well before humans arrived in North America.

Another new area of study relies on *Sporormiella*, a spore often found in animal dung, as a proxy for the presence of megafauna.

At Fordham University in New York, Guy Robinson and colleagues have used *Sporormiella* to study the sequence of events at four sites in southeastern New York. Drilled cores of sediment show that first, levels of *Sporormiella* drop off drastically, suggesting that the megafauna were dying off. Next, fires swept across the area—perhaps a sign that humans had just arrived. Finally, levels of pollen from cool-weather trees spike, suggesting that the cold snap in this region happened after the megafauna were already gone.

"In a way, I feel I've only just scratched the surface," says Robinson, "but it's exposed some intriguing questions."

Such studies may help clarify the extinction puzzle where archaeological remains cannot.

Experts agree, perhaps pessimistically, that they may never know exactly what caused the extinction of North America's great animals.

"It's probably not something that's going to be easy to identify," says Haynes. "The point is, we should still be talking about it."

According to many paleontologists, or "dinosaur hunters," our popular conception of the age of the dinosaurs is in need of a radical revision. The iconic dinosaurs so closely associated with the Cretaceous period—Tyrannosaurus rex, Velociraptor, Triceratops, and others—are, in fact, oddball monsters confined to North America and not representative of the many other creatures that roamed the planet 100 million years ago. New discoveries by paleontologists exploring once-remote regions of the world are changing our view of dinosaur communities. In the last decade, scientists working in South America and Africa, in particular, have found truly gargantuan sauropods, a carnivore bigger than T. rex, and primitive-looking creatures that seem to belong to an even earlier age. These creatures, neither T. rex nor Velociraptor, dominated the Cretaceous period. Fascinating and thrilling in themselves, these new discoveries also remind us that science is not a stable discipline. It shifts with every new discovery, every new theory, and every new researcher entering the field. —KH

"Here Be Monsters"
by Graham Lawton
New Scientist, **September 23, 2000**

If it's September, then it must be time for Paul Sereno to leave civilisation behind and go looking for dinosaurs. This year, the University of Chicago palaeontologist is contemplating four months in Niger's Tenere desert, a vast arc of wilderness stretching from the Algerian border to the heart of the Sahara. Tenere is so remote that even geographers call it "the desert within a desert." To get there, Sereno's team will have to strike out across open dunes in four-wheel-drive trucks, tracking their progress by global positioning satellites and hauling their water supply behind them. It's hardly well-worn dinosaur territory, but that's the point. Sereno isn't looking for well-worn dinosaurs. He's hoping for oddballs, like the three he dug up last time he went to Niger. And he reckons he'll find them, no trouble.

Sereno is not alone. From South America to Madagascar, dinosaur hunters are unearthing creatures from the Cretaceous period—the third and final part of the dinosaur era, from 144 to 65 million years ago—that are startlingly different from those we have come to think of as "normal." The animals they're digging up—and the ones that don't seem to be there to be dug up—are giving us a much clearer idea of what the world was like as the age of the dinosaurs drew to a close. And it turns out that what most of us think of as classic Cretaceous dinosaurs were actually nothing of the sort. In fact, they were regional specialities, confined to a small corner of the northern hemisphere. It's as if today's zoologists had focused on Australia and concluded that kangaroos and koalas were the dominant forms of non-human life on Earth.

Open a child's dinosaur book and chances are you'll be presented with three world views, corresponding to the three great divisions of the dinosaur age. First comes the Triassic, with primitive monsters such as Plateosaurus and sail-backed, snaggle-toothed Dimetrodon (not actually a dinosaur, but a mammal-like reptile). Then there's the Jurassic and its familiar beasts: giant, long-necked sauropods like Diplodocus, Apatosaurus (formerly Brontosaurus) and Brachiosaurus, plate-backed plant eaters like Stegosaurus and the 12-metre predator Allosaurus. Last of all the Cretaceous, the climax of the era and home to the icons of the age: Tyrannosaurus rex and Triceratops, sickle-clawed Velociraptor, snorkel-crested Parasaurolophus, club-tailed Ankylosaurus and duck-billed Hadrosaurus.

But these old friends may soon have to step aside. According to researchers like Sereno, the standard view of the Cretaceous is too regionalist, being based entirely on dinosaurs discovered in North America, Mongolia and a few other parts of the northern hemisphere. During the past ten years, he and a group of like-minded researchers have—literally—broken new ground all over the southern continents in search of the hemisphere's lost dinosaurs. Thanks to their efforts, palaeontologists can begin making generalisations about life in these less explored regions. And some of their conclusions are startling.

For one thing, the southern hemisphere seems to have been a land of giants. Africa, for example, was home to a predator larger than T. rex. Argentina had two or three others that were even bigger. Their prey was truly gargantuan: one sauropod from Argentina was the largest land animal ever to walk the Earth.

In other respects, the south was an evolutionary backwater. While life in the northern hemisphere exploded into myriad forms, the southern continents plodded on as normal. "Something extraordinary happened in the north at the beginning of the Cretaceous," says Philip Currie, director of the Royal Tyrrell Museum of Palaeontology in Drumheller, Canada, who has spent time hunting for dinosaurs in Patagonia. "Things happened much more gradually in the southern hemisphere. The dinosaurs there got more sophisticated, but basically we have an extension of the Jurassic."

"It's a divided world," adds Sereno. "There are clear differences between north and south." He should know. The dinosaurs he discovered in Niger in 1997 were so unusual they took more than two years to sort out. First there was Suchomimus, a crocodile-jawed, sail-backed monster that fished the rivers of West Africa 100 million years ago. Then there was Jobaria, a primitive, long-necked giant that was already a "living fossil" when it roamed the swamps 135 million years ago, since it looked 40 million years older. And last of all Nigersaurus, an enigmatic spade-headed herbivore with hundreds of teeth that's so odd-looking even Sereno describes it as "marvellously bizarre." What's more, the region seems devoid of the archetypal

Cretaceous animals. It's as if Sereno had discovered a lost world in the middle of the Sahara.

And in a sense it is a lost world, at least when viewed from the northern hemisphere. For most of the dinosaur era, the world's landmasses were cemented together in a massive supercontinent called Pangaea. Animals that evolved in one part of the world could—and did—spread quickly to others. Bones of the Jurassic predator Allosaurus, for example, have been found all over the world, from the US to Portugal, Australia and Tanzania.

Jurassic Shift

But during the late Jurassic, the world started to change. Continental drift split Pangaea in two and by the early Cretaceous, 140 million years ago, the world's dry land was divided into two continents. To the north lay Laurasia (which is now North America and Eurasia) and to the south, Gondwana (South America, Africa, Madagascar, India, Australia and Antarctica). Rifts continued to develop throughout the Cretaceous, dividing Laurasia in two and splitting the Gondwanan landmass into smaller and smaller chunks.

This fragmentation, of course, stopped dinosaurs from wandering freely all over the world. And that ought to mean that different types of animals evolved in different regions. The most pronounced division should be between Laurasia and Gondwana. Palaeontologists have long acknowledged that this should be the case, but had little evidence to back it up. "There was a feeling that the southern hemisphere was different," says Dale Russell, the senior curator of palaeontology at the North Carolina

State Museum of Natural Sciences in Raleigh, and another Niger veteran. "But the record was very scrappy." Most fossil hunters were content to focus on the rich Cretaceous deposits in Asiamerica, today's western North America and East Asia. Few bothered with the southern hemisphere. As recently as 10 years ago, the five best-known dinosaur faunas all came from Laurasian countries (the US, Mongolia, China, Canada and Britain).

The revision of this world view began in earnest in 1985 when Argentinian palaeontologist Jose Bonaparte unearthed two new flesh-eating dinosaurs in Patagonia. One, Carnotaurus, was a superb specimen, an entire skeleton so well preserved that its skin had left impressions in the surrounding rock. It came from the middle Cretaceous, around 100 million years ago. Yet it was unlike anything ever discovered from that time. For one thing, it had horns above its eyes—hence the name, which means "meat-eating bull." The shape of its brain case—one of the prime diagnostic features of predatory dinosaurs—was unfamiliar. Overall, it looked remarkably primitive. The other species, called Abelisaurus, was incomplete, but it had clear similarities to Carnotaurus. Taken together, the discoveries seemed to suggest that there was an unknown group of bipedal predators roaming Argentina around the time T. rex dominated the northern hemisphere. In fact, Carnotaurus and Abelisaurus were so unusual that palaeontologists assigned them to a wholly new group of dinosaurs, the abelisaurids, part of a lineage that diverged from the main branch of carnivorous dinosaurs around 230 million years ago. More abelisaurids later turned up in India and Madagascar.

Southern Titans

Patagonia, meanwhile, continued to yield enigmatic monsters. In 1991, Bonaparte dug up a titanosaur, a long-necked sauropod herbivore around 24 metres in length. Two years later, he found another species. Though fragmentary, its remains indicated that it was 45 metres long and weighed 100 tonnes, making it the largest animal ever to have walked the Earth. He and his colleague, Rodolfo Coria of the Carmen Funes Museum in Neuquen, called it Argentinosaurus.

Coria himself was also finding spectacular new species. In 1995, this time working with Leonardo Salgado of the Museum of Natural Sciences in Neuquen, he discovered a meat eater that brought Patagonia's dinosaurs to the world's attention. It looked a lot like T. rex, but it was bigger. Giganotosaurus, as they called it, was around 14 metres long and weighed 8 tonnes, making it bigger than even the biggest T. rex, which up to that point had been thought of as the largest predator the world had ever seen. But Giganotosaurus was no match for T. rex in one respect: its brain was about half the size. In March of this year, Coria and Philip Currie announced the discovery of another meat eater that was bigger still. Currie says there are remains of a third Giganotosaurus-like species that dwarfs the lot.

The discoveries add up to an inescapable conclusion: in South America, Cretaceous dinosaurs tended to be bigger, dumber, and more primitive than their northern contemporaries. The most abundant herbivores were long-necked sauropods, a group that died out over most of Laurasia around the beginning of the Cretaceous. The most common predators, meanwhile, were the abelisaurids, dinosaurs that seem to have flourished in isolation on the southern continent and are absent further north. And right at the top of the food chain were monstrous, pea-brained beasts like Giganotosaurus—throwbacks to the allosaurs of an earlier age. "Most South American dinosaur fauna are oversized forms," says Coria. "They represent primitive dinosaurs that were widely distributed around the world during the Jurassic period, but survived another 50 million years into the Cretaceous in South America. This was their last bastion before they went extinct."

Many of the patterns found in Patagonia are repeated elsewhere. Abelisaurids, for example, have turned up in India, Madagascar and Africa. And titanosaurs have now been found all across the southern hemisphere. "Everywhere other than Asiamerica, sauropods are easily the most common dinosaurs," says Thomas Holtz, a palaeontologist at the University of Maryland. That's especially true in Africa. Apart from the titanosaurs, the continent has at least two other groups of sauropod, both discovered in Niger by Sereno. One is Jobaria, the herbivorous "living fossil." The other is Nigersaurus, the spade-headed weirdo. Though Nigersaurus is descended from Diplodocus, the gangly Jurassic sauropod whose skeleton graces the foyer of London's Natural History Museum, it looks very different. It's one of the smallest sauropods on record, reaching only 15 metres in length. And its mouth is stuffed with rows and rows of teeth—as many as 600 per individual. Nigersaurus may have filled the same ecological niche as the duck-billed dinosaurs of Asiamerica. And, according to Sereno, there are hints of a similar species in South America.

Nigersaurus isn't the only odd African herbivore. In 1999, Russell published details of an eccentric creature from Niger called Lurdusaurus ("weighty lizard"). "It's a funny thing," he says. "It's like a hippopotamus, low to the ground, barrel-chested and with a small head. And it's got this powerful thumb claw." Not, in other words, a lot like your regular northern plant-eater.

Africa also has big predators that fit the Gondwanan pattern. On their maiden expedition to Niger, in 1993, Sereno's team unearthed the complete skeleton of a meat eater, the best specimen ever found in Africa. They called it Afrovenator ("African hunter") and assigned it to a group called the torvosauroids. These evolved during the Jurassic but, until 1993, were unknown in the Cretaceous. Two years later the team unearthed two more predators, this time in the Kem Kem region of Morocco. One, Deltadromeus ("delta runner"), was a swift and graceful hunter that seems to have evolved in isolation in Africa. The other, Carcharodontosaurus ("shark-toothed lizard"), was a flesh-guzzling monster that is related to the giants of South America. Carcharodontosaurus could easily have gone toe-to-toe with Giganotosaurus: it was more than 14 metres long and weighed a gargantuan 8 tonnes.

Crocodile Jaws

More finds continued to surface. In 1997, Sereno found another torvosauroid in Niger, the crocodile-jawed

Suchomimus. This was the most common predator of its day. It was at least 11 metres long and had an elongated snout bristling with hook-shaped teeth for snaring fish. In 1998, Russell found traces of a similar creature in Morocco. South America, too, has a crocodile-jawed fish eater, the delightfully named Irritator challengeri. This got its name because the only known skull had been damaged by amateur palaeontologists.

The pictures that are emerging of Africa and South America, then, are strikingly similar. Both were home to giant sauropods and Allosaurus-like predators long after these groups had started to dwindle in Laurasia. And both had eccentric-looking species that evolved in isolation following the split of Pangaea. "You have two sorts of animal," says Sereno. "There are animals that survived only on the southern continents, and there are animals that evolved on the southern continent and are not found elsewhere."

Laurasian Echoes

Within this broad pattern, however, there are some stray threads. The dinosaurs of Australia and Antarctica seem much more like those found in Laurasia. In 1998, for example, a tooth from a duck-billed dinosaur was found in Cretaceous deposits in the Antarctic. "It's a bit of an enigma," says Currie. "Some of the material down there is not like Gondwanan animals. There are some things that are more suggestive of the northern hemisphere." Gondwanan animals have also started showing up in Laurasia. Suchomimus, for example, has a close European relative called Baryonyx, found in early Cretaceous rocks on the Isle of Wight, off England's south coast. The two are so similar that that they may in fact be the same species. What's more, titanosaurs have been uncovered in Western Europe, North America and Mongolia.

"It's a complex picture," says Sereno. "The break-up of Pangaea didn't create insurmountable obstacles to these intrepid explorers." One possible explanation is that land bridges formed from time to time as a result of changes in sea level, temporarily reuniting divided land masses and allowing migration and intermingling of species. Another possibility is that the fossil record simply isn't good enough to give us a complete picture.

Whatever the real reason, Sereno and his fellow explorers are sure that the fossil beds of Gondwana will continue to yield surprises. "There's lots more to come," says Russell. They're also convinced that what they find will continue to marginalise T. rex, Triceratops and the other Laurasian icons. "The dinosaurs of North America and Eurasia were an unusual endemic fauna, real weirdos that were generated in isolation," says Holtz. "Southern hemisphere dinosaurs are the main strand of dinosaur history."

Reprinted with permission from *New Scientist*.

Since we cannot go back and replay the tape of evolution to determine exactly how and why (or even whether) some dinosaurs evolved into birds, paleontologists search rocks for fossil

clues about how the transition may have been achieved. Based on the fossil evidence, some of these paleontologists are now confident that they know which dinosaurs gave rise to exactly what sorts of birds, but fossilized bits of feather and bone have been less helpful in explaining how the act of flying itself evolved. There has been no shortage of theories. Maybe wings first helped their owner to glide and only later to fly. Maybe feathered appendages helped organisms to stay warm or, when spread wide, to snare insects. Researcher Kenneth Dial took a different approach to the question. He turned to some of today's weak fliers—chickens and their relatives—and asked what purpose other than flight their poorly developed wings serve. How do their wings help them in everyday life? The answer is not what you might think, and his experiments demonstrate how out-of-the-box thinking can change the direction of evolutionary science. —KH

"Uphill Flight: A Partridge's Ability to Climb Overhanging Slopes Might Explain How Dinosaurs Took to the Skies"
by Adam Summers
Natural History, December 2003

The debate over the origin of birds has raged through the paleontological community for more than a century.

Fitting species into evolutionary family trees is painstaking and often contentious work, but truly amazing discoveries of feathered fossils in Liaoning Province in northeastern China have enabled paleontologists to identify the group of dinosaurs that gave rise to Tweety and brethren. The fossils, unearthed in the past decade, even give a peek at the origin of feathers. But paleontologists still debate one point: How did bipedal but terrestrial archosaurs (the "old lizards," which include dinosaurs, birds, and crocodilians) learn to flap their arms and fly? Not surprisingly (given the title of this column), biomechanics has come to the rescue. One of the most compelling hypotheses for the evolution of avian flight has recently been well fortified by observing the habits of some of today's poorest fliers.

Two main camps have dominated the debate about the origin of flight. According to the "trees-down" camp, arboreal dinosaurs first evolved the ability to glide off their perch in a tree, much the way colugos— the so-called "flying lemurs"—and some frogs, lizards, snakes, and squirrels do today. Later, the gliders evolved the ability to flap from tree to tree.

Proponents of the trees-down scenario maintain that wings and feathers would have been useful for gliding, even if they preceded such adaptations as the shoulder girdle, the huge pectoral muscles, and the peculiar wrist and hand structures that make possible the powered, flapping flight of birds. Yet, as detractors of the hypothesis point out, none of the extant gliding animals perform even rudimentary flapping. They are all strictly gliders, and there is no reason to suppose they will ever be otherwise. Even worse, the dinosaurs most closely related to birds, the unfeathered dromaeosaurs, which include such terrors as Deinonychus and the better known Velociraptor, were clearly terrestrial. So even though a change from gliding to flapping might be an easy idea to swallow, neither the several independently evolved gliders nor the fossil record lend it any support.

Partisans from the second camp, in contrast, favor a "ground-up" hypothesis. In their view, terrestrial, bipedal dinosaurs flapped their "arms" first and later evolved into fliers. But the ground-up hypothesis has faced an even tougher challenge than the trees-down view. Although the fossil record clearly demonstrates that pre-avian dinosaurs were fond of terra firma, explanations that require the transition from bald, sprinting dinosaur to feathered, flapping bird seem a bit far-fetched. Feathers might have, for example, evolved as insulation, which would further imply that dromaeosaurs were endothermic, or warm-blooded. Or maybe feathered arms were useful as a net to catch flying insects, or as a horizontal stabilizer—like a tightrope-walker's pole—for swiftly running, predatory bipeds.

One biologist has come up with a ground-up proposal that, on the face of it, might seem even more off the wall. Kenneth P. Dial studies the biomechanics of flight at the University of Montana in Missoula. He suggested recently that flight arose from arm movements intended to push a bird (or a feathered dinosaur) into the ground rather than lift it up. The genesis of that odd

idea was his observation that, when running up a slope, a chukar partridge (Alectoris chukar) flaps its wings quite differently than a bird does when it tries to get off the ground.

Partridges, chickens, and quail are known as galliform birds (the name comes from the Latin word *gallus*, meaning "rooster," and the Galliformes are all chicken-like). Typically, they have broad, stubby wings; easily fatigued flight muscles; and chicks that are ready to run, though not to fly, when they hatch. When a predator such as a fox or a weasel threatens a young chukar partridge, the bird escapes by fleeing up a steep slope. As it runs uphill, the chukar flaps its wings madly. The behavior has long been regarded as a failed attempt at flying, pointless because the young chukar's flight feathers (called remiges) are not yet fully developed.

Dial first established that though the remiges are not long enough to enable takeoff, they do improve traction enough for the young chukars to climb. After trimming or removing the remiges of chukars of various ages, Dial discovered that without the help of feathers, the birds could not run up slopes steeper than sixty degrees. Fully feathered animals, however, could scamper and flap their way up vertical and even slightly over-hanging slopes.

Dial then turned his attention to the birds' legs. To measure their contribution to the climb, he constructed two kinds of ramp, smooth and textured, which gave quite different traction to scrabbling claws. No matter how well feathered they were, adult birds and young birds alike couldn't scale smooth ramps steeper than fifty degrees.

The data could be explained in two ways. It might initially seem obvious that the flight feathers, though short on the younger birds, nonetheless provide enough vertical lift to make the chicks light on their feet, boosting them up the steeper slopes. Alternatively, the flapping wings could be generating force in the direction of the ramp, increasing the hind-limb traction of the fleeing chicks. This hypothesis also fits with another observation: the stroke of every chukar's (whether young or old) wing beat while running is quite different than that of its wing beat while flying. Rather than flapping the wings from back to belly, as other birds do, the partridges flap from head to tail.

To test the two hypotheses, Dial and his student Matthew W. Bundle attached a small accelerometer to the back of a bird (the instrument measures the acceleration of the bird's center of mass at any point in time) and filmed the animal running up a ramp. They confirmed that from late in the downstroke through the middle of the upstroke, much of the force generated by the flapping wings helps a chukar's feet get traction.

This research implies a plausible model for the selective advantage of both the flapping motion and a poorly feathered wing. Lightly feathered dromaeosaurs might have relied on wings for help in climbing steep slopes and even entering trees, just as extant galliform birds do. The peculiar flapping style that helps ground the bird could then easily be co-opted into the wing stroke now present in flighted birds. The chukars vary the angle of their wings depending on the slope of the

substrate they're climbing, and the angle becomes increasingly similar to that of a flying bird as a chukar climbs slopes of ninety degrees or steeper.

It's not conclusive evidence for the evolution of flight—and since behavior doesn't fossilize, one can never be certain. For the first time, however, the ground-up proponents have a model that's not so much "off the wall" as up it.

Reprinted from *Natural History* December 2003; copyright © Natural History Magazine, Inc. 2003.

The discovery in October 2004 of bones of miniature people, cousins to modern humans, on the Indonesian island of Flores sent ripples of surprise, excitement, delight, and curiosity throughout the world. No community was more intrigued by the discovery, however, than evolutionary biologists and paleoanthropologists. After the initial excited flush of discovery passed, it became apparent that the Floresians—as the three and a half feet tall human ancestors were called—posed several puzzles that called into question the usual assumptions of human evolution. First of all, evidence suggests that the Floresians were adept toolmakers, fashioning stone weapons in order to hunt the miniature elephants with whom they shared the island. Yet the brain

size of the Floresians was only one-third that of modern humans. This is the same brain size seen in chimpanzees and the Australopithecines, ape-like human ancestors. Neither of whom are thought to be capable of the sophisticated reasoning and comprehension necessary to fashion tools for specific tasks. As a result, there is a difference of opinion whether the Floresians are descended from Homo erectus *(archaic humans) or* Homo sapiens *(modern humans). They seem to have existed on Flores until about 18,000 years ago, meaning they survived for at least 20,000 years after the first appearance of* Homo sapiens *in that part of the world. If the Floresians are descended from* Homo erectus, *that would mean they were the only group of archaic humans to survive into modern times. The Floresians prompt many other evolutionary and anthropological questions: How did they reach Flores? Did they build and sail boats? How did they get smarter as their brain size was actually decreasing? Did they hunt with the help of verbal communication? We are still many years away from any definitive answers to these questions, but until then we can all enjoy the extremely rare opportunity to discover and come to understand a previously unknown branch of the human family tree.* —KH

"Miniature People Add Extra Pieces to Evolutionary Puzzle"
by Nicholas Wade
New York Times, November 9, 2004

The miniature people found to have lived on the Indonesian island of Flores until 13,000 years ago may well appeal to the imagination. Even their Australian discoverers refer to them with fanciful names. But the little Floresians have created something of a headache for paleoanthropologists.

The Floresians, whose existence was reported late last month, have shaken up existing views of the human past for three reasons: they are so recent, so small and apparently so smart. None of these findings fits easily into current accounts of human evolution.

The textbooks describe an increase in human brain size that parallels an increasing sophistication in stone tools. Our close cousins the chimpanzees have brains one third the size of ours, as do the Australopithecines, the apelike human ancestors who evolved after the split from the joint human-chimp ancestor six or seven million years ago. But the Australopithecines left no stone tools, and chimps, though they use natural stones to smash things, have no comprehension of fashioning a stone for a specific task.

The little Floresians seem to have made sophisticated stone tools yet did so with brains of 380 cubic centimeters, about the same size as the chimp and Australopithecine brains. This is a thumb in the eye for the tidy textbook explanations that link sophisticated technology with increasing human brain size.

The Australian and Indonesian researchers who found the Floresian bones have an explanation that raises almost as many questions as it resolves. They say the Floresians, who stood three and a half feet high, are downsized versions of Homo erectus, the archaic humans who left Africa 1.5 million years before modern humans. But some critics think the small people may have descended from modern humans—Homo sapiens.

Homo erectus had arrived on the remote island of Flores by 840,000 years ago, according to earlier findings by Dr. Mike Morwood, the Australian archaeologist on the team. The species then became subject to the strange evolutionary pressures that affect island species. If there are no predators and little food, large animals are better off being small. Homo erectus was sharply downsized, as was the pygmy elephant the little Floresians hunted.

But the Morwood theory is not universally accepted. Homo erectus is known to have made crude stone tools but is not generally thought to have spoken or been able to build boats.

Maybe Dr. Morwood's alleged stone tools were just natural pieces of rock. "Many researchers (myself included) doubted these claims," writes Chris Stringer, a paleoanthropologist at the Natural History Museum in London, adding that "nothing could have prepared me" for the surprise of the little Floresians.

It is surprising enough that Homo erectus managed to reach Flores. But not only have the Floresians evolved to be much more advanced than their ancestors ever were, as judged by the stone tools, but they did so at the same time that their brain was being reduced to one-third human size. Getting smaller brained and smarter at the same time is the exact reverse of the textbook progression.

The Floresians' other surprise lies in the time of their flourishing. The skeleton described in *Nature* lived as recently as 18,000 years ago, but Dr. Morwood said that in the most recent digging season he found six other individuals whose dates range from 95,000 to 13,000 years ago. Modern humans from Africa arrived in the Far East some time after 50,000 years ago and had reached Australia by at least 40,000 years ago.

There has been little evidence until now that Homo erectus long survived its younger cousins' arrival in the region. Modern humans probably exterminated the world's other archaic humans, the Neanderthals in Europe. Yet the little Floresians survived some 30,000 years into modern times, the only archaic human species known to have done so.

All these surprises raise an alternative explanation. What if the Floresians are descended from modern humans, not from Homo erectus?

"I think the issue of whether it derives from H. erectus or H. sapiens is difficult or impossible to answer on the morphology," says Dr. Richard Klein, an archaeologist at Stanford. And if the individual described in the *Nature* articles indeed made the sophisticated tools found in the same cave, "then it is more likely to be H. sapiens," he says.

The same possibility has been raised by two anthropologists at the University of Cambridge, Dr. Marta Mirazón Lahr and Dr. Robert Foley. Commenting on the sophisticated stone implements found in the cave with the Floresians, they write that "their contrast with tools found anywhere with H. erectus is very striking."

There is the basis here for a fierce dispute. Given what is on the record so far, the argument that the Floresians are descended from Homo sapiens, not erectus, has a certain parsimony. Moderns are known to have been around in the general area, and no Homo erectus is known to have made such sophisticated tools.

Dr. Morwood counters this thesis with data that he has not yet published, and which therefore does not strictly count in scientific arguments. The 95,000-year-old Floresians far antedate the arrival of modern humans in the area. There are modern human remains on Flores, Dr. Morwood says, but the earliest is 11,000 years old, suggesting there was not necessarily any overlap between the two human species.

His view is supported by Dr. G. Philip Rightmire, a paleoanthropologist at Binghamton University in New York and an expert on Homo erectus. "There is no ambiguity about the morphological pattern, and it is erectus-like," Dr. Rightmire says of the Floresian skeleton. "I'm not sure why it should be difficult to accept the reasoning that the little Floresians made progress with stone working and honed their hunting-butchering skills" during their long co-existence on Flores with the pygmy elephants, he said.

Dr. Morwood believes the little Floresians must have had language to cooperate in elephant hunts. Others are not willing to follow him so far, especially given Homo erectus's apparent lack of achievement. Even chimps can hunt cooperatively, Dr. Foley says.

Whether the Floresians' line of descent runs through Homo erectus or through Homo sapiens, a whole new line of human evolution has opened up, even though one that is now all but certainly extinct. The Floresians are not like human pygmies, which have almost normal-size brains but smaller bodies because their growth is retarded during puberty. Nor are they dwarves. The skeleton described last month could be called a midget, in the sense of a tiny person with the head and body proportions of a full-size person, Dr. Klein said.

"I always tell my students that I've taught for 30 years and I've never given the same lecture twice. Hardly a year goes by when something new isn't found," says Dr. Leslie Aiello, a paleoanthropologist at University College London. Of the Floresian discovery she says, "It's a total knockout."

*One of the delights of evolution is the impor-
tance of accidents. In evolutionary terms,
accidents are mutations—a usually permanent
change in hereditary material—and they provide the fuel of natural selection. According to
Bob Holmes, a "chaperone" protein called hsp90
appears to let cells tuck away mutations "for a
rainy day," when sudden adaptation is most
needed by organisms in order to survive. When
organisms are faced with extreme adversity, a
whole grooming system moderated by hsp90
breaks down, and helpful mutations that were
once hidden suddenly appear, allowing them to
speed up the pace of evolution and survive
stressful conditions. If these helpful mutations
are inherited by succeeding generations, they
will become permanent, and specieswide
adaptation will have occurred. Some researchers
even think that hsp90 may play an important
role in the aging process. As we age, we accumulate mutations, but our hsp system helps us
suppress any damaging ones. At some point,*

*however, the system becomes overloaded,
and harmful mutations suddenly start to wreak
havoc on our bodies, possibly triggering
diseases such as cancer, heart disease, and
diabetes.* —KH

"Ready, Steady, Evolve"
by Bob Holmes
New Scientist, September 28, 2002

Despite its universal role in biology, evolution still poses some pretty perplexing questions. Take changes in body form. Every tree or beetle or mouse looks the way it does because thousands of genes turned on at exactly the right time and place to guide the organism from single cell to adulthood. But if body plans are the product of such intricately orchestrated programs, how can evolution ever conjure up new ones? Any slight perturbation would surely send a species tumbling from its evolutionary peak into the barren valleys beneath.

Plants and animals may have hit on an ingenious solution—bottling up evolution for times when they really need it. By squirrelling away genetic mutations, the raw material of evolution, and releasing them all at once, species may be able to leap from peak to evolutionary peak without ever having to slog through the valleys between. This happy knack increases their odds of surviving stressful conditions—nothing less than evolution on demand.

On the face of it, the idea sounds like biological heresy. Plants and animals couldn't have that sort of control over the random process underlying evolution, could they?

Surprisingly, they could. Over the past few years, a handful of lab experiments have thrown up convincing evidence that organisms really can save up mutations for a rainy day. If the same thing happens in nature, then plants and animals have hit on a way to seize the throttle of evolution, accelerating it when necessary and slowing it down when not. Their storehouse of mutations may also prove to be a treasure trove of new genes for drug hunters to plunder or, equally, the time-bomb that helps explain the diseases of old age.

The lead actor in this iconoclastic drama is a so-called "chaperone" protein called hsp90. One of the most abundant proteins in animals, plants and fungi, hsp90's job is to bind to unstable proteins and help them maintain their correct shape. In this role, hsp90 is rather like a valet, tidying up proteins that would otherwise become dishevelled by environmental insults such as high temperatures. Hence the chaperones' other name, "heat shock proteins."

But hsp90 is also a crucial regulator of development. As a way of silencing proteins until their services are required, cells deliberately make some proteins unstable, especially certain ones that regulate developmental pathways. One of hsp90's jobs is to hold some of these proteins in the "standby" position. "It works on just about every [developmental] pathway you can imagine," says Susan Lindquist, director of the Whitehead Institute for Biomedical Research in Cambridge, Massachusetts.

The first hint that hsp90's job gives it unusual leverage over evolution came four years ago, when Lindquist and her team mate Suzanne Rutherford were working at the University of Chicago. They noticed that fruit flies carrying a mutant copy of the hsp90 gene sometimes had offspring that looked very weird indeed. "We had eyes that grew out from the head in a stalk-like pattern, we had bristles in the wrong places, wings with different venation patterns and shapes, abdomens that were partly folded over, legs that were different shapes—virtually every structure in the adult fly was affected," says Lindquist. The same abnormalities showed up in normal flies doped in the larval stage with geldanamycin, a drug that interferes with the action of hsp90 (*Nature*, vol 396, p 336).

That wasn't too surprising, given hsp90's pivotal role in development. But when the researchers looked more closely at their abnormal flies, they saw something much more interesting: each set of parents tended to produce offspring with a distinctive set of abnormalities, different from those in unrelated fly lineages. One might have deformed legs, another strangely positioned eyes and stunted wings. If the flies' bizarre body plans were simply down to a shortage of hsp90 playing havoc with their developmental pathways, then the defects should have been scattered randomly throughout the whole fly population. But they weren't.

There was something else going on, and the researchers thought they knew what it was. They suggested that the familial abnormalities were caused by "cryptic" genetic defects that had lain hidden for generations and only showed up when hsp90 stopped doing its job. That would explain why each lineage sported a different set of abnormalities: each one had its own, unique collection of hidden defects.

This makes sense given hsp90's way of working. When all is well, the researchers proposed, hsp90 goes about its usual business of keeping unstable proteins in working order. It does this so efficiently that it can even tuck into shape proteins with minor mutations that would otherwise alter their shape and, therefore, their functions. In effect, hsp90 papers over the flaws in an organism's genome by keeping mutations hidden harmlessly away—including mutations in the genes that regulate development. Over the generations, a lineage of flies can accumulate many minor mutations that never see the light of day.

In times of stress, though, this patina of orderliness breaks down. High temperatures, noxious chemicals, and a host of other stresses can cause an epidemic of protein misfolding. Faced with a dramatically increased workload, hsp90 can no longer keep up and, as a result, malformed proteins go unrepaired. That means stress can lead to the sudden unmasking of hidden mutations. If it happens during larval development or metamorphosis, hidden mutations in developmental genes can produce abrupt changes in shape and form.

Remarkably, then, hsp90 acts as both a capacitor for storing genetic variation and the trigger that releases it. It therefore gives evolutionary biologists a convincing molecular explanation for evolutionary change. "This looks like something that's going to put evolutionary theory on a firmer ground in terms of mechanism," says Massimo Pigliucci, an evolutionary ecologist at the University of Tennessee in Knoxville.

Earlier this year, Lindquist's team announced that hsp90 performs the same trick in the thale cress, *Arabidopsis thaliana*—making it likely that many other organisms store variation in this way, too. Once again, drugs that interfere with hsp90 caused some seedlings to develop abnormally. "We had roots that grew up instead of down, changes in the number of root hairs, leaves that developed almost like pine needles, leaves that curled up or down, leaves that became pigmented—all sorts of things," says Lindquist. Many of the variants looked as if they might be helpful to plants trying to adapt to new environments—more or fewer root hairs, for example, might be appropriate for different soil types and moisture conditions—though the researchers did not test this directly. Again, different inbred lines of the plants produced seedlings with different sets of abnormalities, and they showed the same characteristic abnormalities when grown at higher temperatures, even without the drug (*Nature*, vol 417, p 618). Hsp90 seemed to be concealing cryptic mutations in plants, too.

What's more, once these new variants come out of the woodwork, the useful ones are likely to stick around even after the environmental stress has disappeared. When Lindquist's team bred fruit flies while selecting for certain abnormalities, after just a few generations the flies hung onto their new shapes even when hsp90 was at full function again. Lindquist believes that selecting for these traits, which are the result of many genes working together, prompts the selected lines to accumulate more and more of the desirable gene variants, until eventually the flies exceed a threshold where the trait becomes independent of hsp90. That's important, because it means organisms won't lose useful mutations once the stress evaporates.

The upshot of this is that species seem to have a mechanism for delivering variation—the raw material of evolution—just at the time they need to adapt to a changing environment. "It's almost too good to be true. Just when you need variation, it's there," says Charles Knight, an evolutionary physiologist at the Max Planck Institute for Chemical Ecology in Jena, Germany.

Maybe so, but Lindquist's results actually sit quite snugly with existing theories of evolution and development. As early as the 1940s, British biologist C. H. Waddington suggested that organisms must have ways of buffering mutations that could disrupt their development. Though Waddington had some experimental evidence, many biologists remained sceptical, because no one knew how such buffering could arise. Lindquist's work provides the first molecular explanation. "The hsp90 work came as a real surprise," says Brian Hall, an evolutionary developmental biologist at Dalhousie University in Halifax, Nova Scotia. "Here's this molecule we've known about for quite some time that could play this really fascinating role."

Hsp90's ability to store and release mutations also helps resolve a long-standing evolutionary puzzle—how species can make the transition from one body plan to another when intermediate forms would seem to be dangerously maladapted. By storing genetic variation and releasing it all at once, a species may be able to muster the raw material for big evolutionary leaps. These larger leaps could increase a species' chances of finding a design that's better adapted to its new conditions, says Lindquist. It may even have been one of the driving forces behind some of the bursts of rapid diversification found in the fossil record—the so-called "punctuated equilibrium" model of evolution popularised by the late palaeontologist Stephen Jay Gould.

For all the advantages of such a system, though, Lindquist has backed away from the suggestion—which she and Rutherford hinted at in their first paper—that this storage-and-release mechanism might have been shaped for that purpose by natural selection. "We're not by any means saying that it evolved for the sake of evolvability," she says now.

Most other researchers agree. "It's actually very difficult to think up cases in which systems evolve in order to make evolution more efficient," says Nicholas Barton, an evolutionary geneticist at the University of Edinburgh. "It's not impossible that that sort of thing can happen, but it takes careful argument to justify it." Instead, hsp90's buffering ability most likely arose as an incidental by-product of its main role in protecting proteins against environmental stress.

But buffering you from genetic mutation may in the end have a less desirable side effect too: one researcher suggests that overloading your chaperone system as you get older may be one cause of the diseases of ageing (see [original article for reference to] "The shock of the old").

While Lindquist's experiments have focused on hsp90, it is unlikely to be the only protein playing this evolutionary game. "I think this is the tip of the iceberg. There are going to be many things that buffer genetic variation," says Lindquist. Hsp90 is just one of a whole platoon of heat shock proteins, and other molecules may also act in similar ways. Earlier this year, for example, researchers at the University of Valencia reported that an hsp dubbed GroEL can repress harmful mutations in the bacterium E. coli (*Nature*, vol 417, p 398).

Though even sceptics say her experiments are impeccable and the buffering mechanism she describes is fascinating, Lindquist herself wouldn't claim organisms necessarily enjoy these payoffs in the real world. "For actual long-term evolution to occur, first of all one of the phenotypes that's uncovered needs to be beneficial," says University of Chicago biologist Martin Feder. Then it has got to hang around long enough to shed its dependency on hsp and become abundant in the population. That means the organism expressing it must find a mate whose genes allow this trait to appear. "While not impossible, these events are fairly improbable," Feder concludes.

Then, too, fruit flies and thale cress are hardly typical of most species in the wild. Besides their many generations of adaptation to life in the lab, these two species became geneticists' favourites partly because of their unusually short life cycles, which means they accumulate mutations more quickly than other plants or animals. More sedate species might never gather enough hidden mutations for this mechanism to be important. "It's possible that the role of heat shock proteins may be overestimated in organisms that reproduce that fast," says Pigliucci.

Nor is it clear that providing more variation will actually prompt organisms to evolve faster. Most natural populations already express ample genetic variation to support evolution, argues Barton: "Even if heritable variation were much lower than it really is, we would be able to account for evolution. You don't have to suppose that organisms are sitting around waiting for variability to come up." As evidence, he notes that if you select organisms for almost any trait you choose, they'll respond—and faster than you usually see evolution proceed in the fossil record.

These will remain open questions until someone can use the hsp system to produce useful adaptations. Feder says he and Lindquist have talked about trying this critical experiment on yeast, but their plans got pushed aside during Lindquist's recent move from Chicago to Massachusetts.

No matter how important hsp90's masking of mutations turns out to be in real-world evolution, Lindquist's experiments seem certain to provide other scientists with a valuable tool. Plant breeders, for example, may be able to expose the hidden variation within a crop species as an alternative to costly and time-consuming techniques such as genetic engineering and cross-breeding with wild relatives. Developmental geneticists may be able to use a similar approach to pick apart the evolution of development. Hall, for example, plans to see whether he can uncover hidden variation in a vertebrate, the dwarf African frog. If so, he hopes to use drugs to block hsp90 at different stages of the frog's life cycle to gauge the variation at each stage.

Such a snapshot, he thinks, would reveal which developmental stages allow the most leeway for innovation and which are most conservative.

All in all, Lindquist's results have evolutionary biologists buzzing. "This could open the floodgates to a lot of follow-up," says Pigliucci. Not a bad yield from a bunch of deformed fruit flies.

Reprinted with permission from *New Scientist*.

Rare is the biology student who has never heard of Britain's famous peppered moths. Within a relatively brief period of time, they have allegedly changed their color from pale pepper to black and back to peppered again in response to Industrial Age pollution and then the cleaner skies of a more environmentally friendly era. However, recent reviews of the original biologists' work on the peppered moths and interviews with contemporary researchers have revealed serious problems with the research. The beautiful photographs of dark and light moths against lichen backgrounds feature dead insects, posed artfully, and at least one author has suggested that an insecure graduate student felt pressured by an overbearing thesis adviser to fudge data. Some biologists—and creationists—argue that the flaws in the original peppered moth research

are fatal, and this so-called textbook example of evolution ought to be deleted from biology books. Others believe the experiments were undertaken in good faith, but there were errors in their execution and the results and conclusions were oversimplified. This debate is likely to continue for some time, but meanwhile, biologists are following up the moth research and continuing to discover other striking examples of rapid, "real-time" evolution. —KH

"Staple of Evolutionary Teaching May Not Be a Textbook Case"
by Nicholas Wade
New York Times, June 18, 2002

A leading example of evolution given in biology textbooks has come unglued, evoking jeers and jubilation in the camp of creationists, who have been trying for years to expel Darwin from the classroom.

The case is that of the peppered moth, which over the course of a few decades has changed its wing color from pale-peppered to black and back to peppered again in parallel with the rise and fall of industrial pollution.

The moth, a furtive citizen of Britain and the United States, flies only at night. During the day, it supposedly hides on the trunks of lichen-encrusted trees, where the normal pale form is almost invisible.

Textbook writers have long held that the dark form of the moth grew much more common when soot from industrial activity blackened the trees and killed the lichens, making the pale form more conspicuous to birds. But with the passage of clean air laws, the lichens returned, the pale form regained its camouflage, and the black form reverted to rarity.

This account of events became an instant hit with Darwinian advocates. The story caught evolution in unusually speedy action, and flagged bird predation as the mechanism of natural selection that drove it. The moths made a striking illustration because in a typical pair of photographs, one with lichen covering a tree trunk and the other with soot, the reader could hardly spot the pale moth in the first or the dark form in the second, and it was easy to imagine a bird being similarly deceived.

For generations of biologists reared on the peppered moth story as perfect proof of Darwin's theory, it came as a shock to learn of certain problems the textbooks ignored and which a new book is interpreting in sinister light.

For one thing, the moths in the famous photos were not alive. Like the parrot in the Monty Python skit, they were ex-moths, winged members of the choir invisible, firmly glued or pinned to their perches.

And they were glued in place for good reason: the peppered moth almost never rests on tree trunks, its preferred hideaway probably being under twigs in the high canopy of trees.

"My own reaction resembles the dismay attending my discovery, at the age of 6, that it was my father and not Santa who brought the presents on Christmas Eve," wrote Dr. Jerry A. Coyne, an evolutionary biologist at the University of Chicago, in a 1998 review of a book, "Melanism: Evolution in Action," which noted the moth photos were staged.

But not everyone sees the peppered moth story as a black-and-white case of deception. Dr. Michael Majerus, a moth man at Cambridge University in England and the author of the book reviewed by Dr. Coyne, is a staunch supporter of the textbook version, despite all the flaws he laid out. So too are American moth experts like Dr. Bruce S. Grant of the College of William and Mary.

The moth's defenders concede that there were serious design problems with the original peppered moth experiments, conducted from the mid-1950's onward by Dr. Bernard Kettlewell of Oxford University. But they say that he and his successors have tried in good faith to correct the problems and that the basic story holds up.

True, many biologists who tested Dr. Kettlewell's findings, though not Dr. Kettlewell himself, used dead moths to test birds' feeding preferences, but it was not done with intent to deceive, and the textbook writers who omitted the detail are at fault for oversimplifying, Dr. Majerus said. "Many of Kettlewell's experiments were not perfect," he said, "but I think they were right qualitatively."

Dr. Theodore D. Sargent of the University of Massachusetts has a less forgiving interpretation. He believes that Dr. Kettlewell's experiments created an entirely artificial situation, with moths in an unnatural position and birds that quickly learned they were being served a free lunch in the woods.

Dr. Sargent is a central figure in "Of Moths and Men," by Judith Hooper, to be published by Norton in August. Ms. Hooper portrays the poisonous relationship between Dr. Kettlewell and his eccentric supervisor at Oxford, E. B. Ford, known as Henry.

"Sensitive to slights and always desperately insecure, Bernard became increasingly intimidated by Henry's basilisk gaze and his nuanced but lacerating put-downs," she writes on evidence from Dr. Kettlewell's son David. Both Dr. Kettlewell and Dr. Ford, like the moths in the pictures, are departed.

Reflecting Dr. Sargent's deep skepticism, Ms. Hooper suggests Dr. Kettlewell may have fudged his peppered moth counts so as to please his overbearing mentor. "I wouldn't want to go on record as saying he cooked his results," she said in an interview, but the failure by others to confirm some of Dr. Kettlewell's findings was "quite damning."

But Dr. Majerus rejected the notion that the two biologists had ever fudged their experiments, noting that he had trained with their students and never heard any suggestion of improper scientific behavior.

Creationists have not been downcast at the confusion in the evolutionists' ranks, assailing the peppered moth story as another typical myth from the fairy tale book of evolution.

And Dr. Jonathan Wells, who belongs to the "intelligent design" school, which sees a designer giving a helping hand to evolution, argued that the case should no longer be presented as a textbook example of evolution in action.

"Part of my gripe with evolutionary biologists is that they make their case sound so much stronger than it really is, and I would prefer to see a good deal more agnosticism," said Dr. Wells, a member of the Discovery Institute in Seattle with doctorates in biology and religious studies.

Perhaps the present truth about the peppered moth is too complicated for textbook treatment. The famous photographs are certainly misleading without mention that they are staged. But the creationists are crowing too early.

The pale form of the peppered moth clearly gave way to the dark, or melanic, form as industrialization and air pollution increased in England and the United States. Biologists agree that one form of the moth's color-determining gene became more common than the other. The process then reversed in the two countries, a compelling example of evolution in action, after clean air laws reduced pollution.

But in some areas the pale moths returned to prominence before the lichens that Dr. Kettlewell argued were their camouflage.

Both Dr. Majerus and Dr. Grant remain convinced that the principal mechanism whereby natural selection acts on the peppered moth is predation by birds, and the two are working hard to prove it before the melanic form disappears altogether.

Dr. Majerus is spending 100 days this year on a bird and peppered moth feeding experiment. Dr. Grant, though now retired, is also in pursuit. From a phone booth in Alaska, where he is hunting for peppered moths, he said the role of lichens had been overemphasized and that grime alone had probably been enough to give the black form of the moth its transient advantage.

In retrospect, biologists may have accepted the simple version of the peppered moth story too eagerly. The Kettlewell experiments on lichen camouflage may have been just an enormous diversion. But the melanic form of the moth did rise and fall, for whatever reason. The moth is no myth, and the moth men's continuing efforts may one day get it ready for evolutionary prime time again.

This New York Times article describes a clear-cut and, to many scientists, beautiful demonstration of evolution at work. Rock pocket mice live in the deserts of the American Southwest. To avoid capture by predatory owls, these mice, most of whom live among buff-colored rocks, have over the ages developed beige fur, which acts as a sort of camouflage. In desert areas covered by ancient lava, however, researchers have discovered that the rock pocket mice have developed dark fur to match the blackened rocks, providing even stronger evidence of natural selection at work. This discovery has been celebrated as the first known

demonstration of a natural evolutionary force (nocturnal predation) inspiring genetic changes that, in turn, lead to an adaptive change. As the New York Times *reports, the rock pocket mouse is likely to become the mammalian counterpart to the classic peppered moth. It is to be hoped, however, that the study's results will hold up better under the intense scrutiny of fellow biologists than those of the initial peppered moth research.* —KH

"The Evolving Peppered Moth Gains a Furry Counterpart"
by Carol Kaesuk Yoon
New York Times, June 17, 2003

In the deserts of the Southwest, among the towering saguaros and the spiny cholla cactuses, rock pocket mice hop and dash in search of a meal of seeds. But while these mice may seem to scamper haphazardly across the desert floor, their arrangement in nature is strikingly orderly.

Nearly everywhere these mice are sandy-colored, well camouflaged as they scurry across beige-colored outcrops. But in some areas, ancient lava flows have left behind swaths of blackened rock. There the same species of rock pocket mouse has only dark coats, having evolved an entirely distinct and, for their surroundings, equally well-disguised pelage.

Now, in a recent study in *The Proceedings of the National Academy of Sciences*, researchers report identifying the gene responsible for the evolution of dark coat coloration in these mice, pinpointing the DNA sequence changes that underlie this classic story of evolutionary change, the cute and furry counterpart to the famous case of the peppered moth.

Researchers say the study is the first documentation of the genetic changes underlying an adaptive change where the evolutionary forces were natural. Scientists point out that other well-known cases involve evolution caused by humans; some have suggested that those changes may be atypical of natural evolutionary change, since they have typically involved intense, directed pressures destroying most of a population, like the spraying of pesticides or the application of antibiotics.

"This work is very important," said Dr. Mike Majerus, an evolutionary geneticist at Cambridge University, who was not part of the study. "Here man is just not involved. The sandy and lava flow substrates are entirely natural phenomena."

Other well-studied examples of human-driven adaptive change include the evolution of pesticide resistance in insects after widespread spraying and the increase in the numbers of dark-winged forms compared with light-winged forms of the peppered moth in the United States and England after industrialization turned air sooty and polluted.

Dr. Michael W. Nachman, a population geneticist, along with colleagues at the University of Arizona, Dr. Hopi E. Hoekstra and Susan L. D'Agostino, studied mice living on Arizona's Pinacate lava flow in Arizona and on light-colored rocks nearby. The researchers were able to take advantage of decades of meticulous work in which other scientists identified some 80 genes that affected coat color in laboratory mice.

On close examination, the light-colored rock pocket mice could be seen to have a type of hair coloration similar to standard, sandy-colored laboratory mice. In this pattern, known as agouti, the hair is black at the base, yellow in the middle and black again at the tip. The dark-colored rock pocket mice had completely dark hairs.

Researchers knew that mutations in a few well-known coat coloration genes in laboratory mice could cause such complete darkening of the hair, and they began by looking at two genes known as agouti and Mc1r. When they looked at DNA sequences in light and dark mice, changes in the agouti gene did not appear to be associated with light-colored fur versus dark-colored. Still, the researchers found that a certain cluster of mutations at Mc1r could be found in every dark-colored mouse.

"It's a textbook story," Dr. Nachman said. "Now we have all the pieces of the puzzle together in a natural setting."

Dr. Nachman noted that while the new study points to the Mc1r gene as the key to turning mice dark on the Pinacate lava flow, the team also found that dark mice on another lava flow in New Mexico did not share those mutations.

"So the same dark color has evolved independently in the two different populations," he said, "through different genetic solutions to the same evolutionary problem." Dr. Nachman said changes in another gene, perhaps the agouti gene, could be responsible for dark coloration in the New Mexico's Pedro Armendaris lava flow.

One could easily imagine that coloration would be of no consequence to the rock pocket mice, as they are nocturnal, darting about under the desert night sky. But researchers, working early in the last century, released light and dark mice on light and dark backgrounds in an enclosure at night and found that owls, a major predator of mice, could easily spot a mouse on a mismatched background.

Dr. Nachman noted, however, that these early researchers did not use rock pocket mice in their study, but instead used a species in which the dark and light forms were actually much less distinct.

As a result, he said, "we think the owls are discriminating even more strongly in our species." He said tiny bits of rock pocket mouse were often found in pellets at owl roosts.

Dr. Majerus said many kinds of animals showed light and dark forms, from deer mice to squirrels and chipmunks. There are even black ladybugs.

"A lot of the dark forms show an association with a particular type of substrate they're on, or the frequency of burning and charring of the trees in the woodlands," he said, noting that it would be interesting to do genetic studies in other animals, to see how many genetic solutions these other animals have come up with to turn dark.

But while many dark forms are abundant and can be studied at scientists' leisure, Dr. Majerus said that of the peppered moth was slowly disappearing.

So while there is nearly unanimous praise for the increasingly clean air in industrialized regions of the United States and Britain, there may be, at least for some scientists, a downside. "We've got about 15 or 16 years," Dr. Majerus said, "before those black forms, if they continue to disappear at the current rate, disappear completely."

In the sober and dry prose typical of eminent science journals, this article describes a truly bizarre experiment in evolutionary biology, one that involves male snakes "pretending" to be female. Biologists had long explained the behavior of such "she-male" snakes as an example of sexual selection rather than natural selection: they reasoned that the behavior was actually competitive and must help the she-males mate with the true female snakes. If she-males could confuse other males crowded in a mating ball around a true female, maybe the she-male could sneak in without attracting competitive attention and "steal" a mating with the female. The authors of this article were

unconvinced by this theory and wondered if straightforward natural selection might actually be a simpler explanation for she-maleness. They came up with an elegant, two-step test of their theory. Their conclusion: natural selection appears to win again. She-male snakes seem to use their fake female hormones to attract warm males. The heat of the deceived males allows the she-males to warm up after hibernation, which in turn reduces their vulnerability to predation by crows. So their mimicking of female snakes is, in fact, a survival strategy they have developed that gives them an evolutionary edge over other male snakes. —KH

"Benefits of Female Mimicry in Snakes"
by R. Shine, B. Phillips, H. Waye, M. LeMaster, and R. T. Mason
Nature, November 15, 2001

Males of several animal species mimic females either in appearance or in the chemical cues they release,[1,2] and this mimicry has generally been interpreted in terms of alternative mating strategies—for example, a male that mimics a female may obtain stolen inseminations or avoid aggression from larger rivals.[3] Our studies of snakes suggest a different explanation, which relies on natural selection rather than sexual selection. Male garter snakes that produce female-like pheromones (she-males) may benefit simply because large "mating balls" of amorous males form around them, transferring heat to the she-male after it emerges from hibernation and reducing its exposure to predators.

Garter snakes (*Thamnophis sirtalis parietalis*) in Manitoba, Canada, court and mate in large aggregations centred around overwintering dens. It has been suggested that the advantage of mimicry lies in a she-male's ability to confuse other males within the mating balls (which sometimes contain more than 100 males) that form around genuine females[2], but she-maleness has since been shown to be a transitory phase that is restricted to the first day or two after a male first emerges from his eight-month hibernation.[4, 5] The snakes are weak and slow at this time and are therefore highly vulnerable to attack by crows.[6] We have identified no mating advantage to she-males,[4] and propose an alternative explanation for female mimicry in this species.

The primary purpose of males producing female pheromones is to attract courtship from other males; indeed, most she-males are virtually obscured by the bodies of their suitors. At a den near Inwood, Manitoba,[5] 49 of 53 newly emerged she-males were partly covered by other males when sighted; overall, an average of 58% of the body of each she-male was covered by other males, whereas only 32 of 55 he-males (at more than 2 days after emergence; none of these was courted) were partly obscured, with an average of 25% cover. She-maleness may benefit newly emerged animals (which are cold, weak and slow[4]) for two reasons. First, a snake hidden beneath other individuals may be less vulnerable to attack by crows.[6-8] Second, courting males press vigorously against the object of their affections[9] and may thus transfer heat—newly emerged snakes are cool (ground temperature is below 10°C), but reproductive males are on average warmer than 25°C. (ref. 10). Courtship could thus increase a she-male's body temperature and therefore his locomotor capacity,[11] as well as accelerating his recovery from hibernation. Many dens are deeply shaded and smooth-sided, making it difficult for a newly emerged snake to bask in sunlight. Because reproductive males travel constantly back and forth between the den and surrounding clearings, however, a snake that attracts courtship will be covered in hot males as soon as it emerges.

Does a cold snake warm up faster if it is courted by hot males? To test this idea, we glued miniature thermal data-loggers (Thermochron I-buttons, Dallas Semiconductors) to the mid-dorsal surfaces of 24 females, which we placed in open-topped outdoor arenas measuring 1×1×1 m (ref. 4). Six arenas contained only four females each, whereas the others contained four females plus twenty males. The average temperature of females was 4°C and that of males was 25°C when we commenced the trials at 11:00 h to mimic newly emerging snakes. The females were heated to 20°C within 30 min, with courted snakes heating faster than uncourted animals.

To verify that this effect was due to heat transfer rather than to courtship-induced changes in the behaviour of courted animals, we repeated the study using dead snakes as the courtship "targets," with thermistor leads implanted to measure deep-body temperature. Again, snakes exposed to courtship were heated faster than those that were not. The thermal benefit from courtship often exceeded 3°C.

Do higher temperatures accelerate recovery from hibernation? We investigated this possibility by capturing she-males soon after they emerged, and then keeping them either warm (28°C) or cool (10°C). At 90-min intervals, we brought five she-males from each group to 25°C and then held them by their tails in the den to quantify their sexual attractiveness. We scored the responses by five mate-searching males to each she-male, using a four-point scale.[4] 'Warm' she-males regained their he-male status within 3 hours, whereas 'cool' snakes remained as she-males for over 5 hours. The intensity of courtship that she-males attracted from other males therefore decreased more rapidly in snakes that were kept warmer.

We conclude that alternative male mating strategies such as female mimicry might have evolved through natural selection (for thermoregulation and predator defence), rather than through sexual selection, as has generally been surmised.[1-3] She-male garter snakes may therefore manipulate their rivals' behaviour not to "steal" matings, but to warm up and to reduce their own vulnerability to predation. Although intuition would favour an interpretation that female mimicry has evolved within the context of alternative mating tactics, simpler explanations should also be investigated.

1. Andersson, M. *Sexual Selection* (Princeton Univ. Press, Princeton, New Jersey, 1994).
2. Mason, R. T. & Crews, D. *Nature* 316, 59–60 (1985).
3. Trivers, R. L. *Evolution* 30, 253–269 (1976).
4. Shine, R., Harlow, P. S., LeMaster, M. P., Moore, I. & Mason, R. T. *Anim. Behav.* 59, 349–359 (2000).
5. Shine, R., O'Connor, D. & Mason, R. T. *Can. J. Zool.* 78, 1391–1396 (2000).
6. Shine, R., LeMaster, M. P., Moore, I. T., Olsson, M. M. & Mason, R. T. *Evolution* 55, 598–604 (2001).
7. Olson, D. H. *Copeia* 1989, 391–397 (1989).
8. Hamilton, W. D. *J. Theor. Biol.* 31, 295–311 (1971).
9. Whittier, J. M., Mason, R. T. & Crews, D. *Behav. Ecol. Sociobiol.* 16, 257–261 (1985).
10. Shine, R., Harlow, P. S., Elphick, M. J., Olsson, M. M. & Mason, R. T. *Physiol. Biochem. Zool.* 73, 508–516 (2000).
11. Heckrotte, C. *Copeia* 1967, 759–763 (1967).

Ticking away in the DNA (deoxyribonucleic acid) of every organism are molecular clocks that record the passage of time by the number of mutations that occur rather than seconds, minutes, or years. By studying mutations, scientists have discovered detailed and accurate records of the emergence of new genes. This article describes one particular search through genomic history for information that could someday help fight malaria, a disease that kills millions of people every year. Researchers have made fascinating and complex discoveries in the genomes of people, mosquitoes (carriers of malaria), and the parasites that cause malaria. Malaria was apparently in existence millions of years ago, but it was not until the last few thousand years that it became a deadly disease. The researchers have zeroed in on the time period when the disease became deadly by identifying the sudden appearance of two mutations in human populations that gave people some level of protection against a newly life-threatening disease. —KH

"The Seeds of Malaria: Recent Evolution Cultivated a Deadly Scourge"
by Ben Harder
Science News, November 10, 2001

The statistics are grim. The parasites that cause malaria infect 300 to 500 million people annually. As many as 3 million of these will die of the disease this year, making it humanity's deadliest infection. Nearly half the world's population lives in countries where malaria epidemics occur, and as the parasites' resistance to drugs grows, the toll is expected to steadily worsen.

How this mosquito-borne disease became the menace it is—and how it continues to get the better of both the human immune system and modern medicine— has puzzled researchers struggling to understand and control malaria. Its evolutionary relationship with people is of more than academic interest. Understanding the history of malaria and the conditions from which it arose could give scientists an edge in finding new therapies.

The single-celled protozoan *Plasmodium falciparum*, the most deadly of four Plasmodium species that cause human malaria, has preyed on people as far back as the human race's evolutionary split with chimpanzees 6 to 10 million years ago. Molecular geneticists, however, are finding evidence that malaria's devastating impact is a relatively recent phenomenon. New findings also hint that the disease is more lethal today than it was just a few thousand years ago.

People have evolved a variety of defenses in response to malaria's threat, and the pace of that evolution gives researchers insight into when the threat arose.

Theorists propose that various genetic mutations among certain groups of people are linked to malaria. These mutations occur almost exclusively in regions where the disease historically has been a killer, and each seems to protect against the infection in one way or another.

Most of these malaria-protective mutations also have a downside, causing blood disorders such as sickle cell anemia and thalassemia. Natural selection would be expected to filter out these mutations or at least keep them at very low frequencies unless their effects in opposing malaria balanced out losses from genetic disease. Scientists call this process "balancing selection."

At least one such disease appears to have cropped up in the past few millennia, according to a recent study conducted by Sarah A. Tishkoff of the University of Maryland in College Park and her colleagues. This implies that malaria earlier on wasn't a sufficiently serious cause of mortality to maintain the mutation through balancing selection.

The researchers examined a series of genetic mutations widespread in regions that show endemic malaria. They appear in the gene responsible for production of an enzyme known as glucose-6-phosphate-dehydrogenase, or G6PD. The mutations can cause G6PD deficiency and result in life-threatening anemia.

The Maryland-led researchers examined the highly variable gene in 605 people from 10 African and 5 non-African populations. The group catalogued the variants, or alleles, of the gene that the participants possess.

Tishkoff's team focused on two alleles that cause G6PD deficiency. Known as Med and A-, these variants appear in Mediterranean and Africa populations, respectively. The researchers looked closely at the DNA flanking each variant.

If either mutation had occurred long ago and been maintained by balancing selection, DNA differences would have accumulated around different copies of each allele. The researchers, however, found few differences in this neighboring DNA among people sharing a variant. This suggests that little time has elapsed since Med and A- arose in the human genome.

Applying a molecular-clock technique based on a predicted rate at which differences accumulate, the researchers estimate the age of A- at between 3,840 and 11,760 years. The Med allele, they suggest, goes back just 1,600 to 6,640 years.

Since natural selection would maintain Med and A- alleles only under conditions of severe malaria, the timing of the alleles' appearance presumably corresponds to the rise in human mortality from the disease. That could have been within the past 12,000 years in Africa and even more recently in Europe. Earlier, Tishkoff infers, the disease must have been significantly less common, less lethal, or both.

What caused malaria's terrible transformation? Any one or a combination of several biological factors could have played a role. An evolving parasite, perhaps with novel adaptations that permit the cells to evade immune detection, might have made the disease more deadly or caused it to spread more easily among people. Changing mosquito behavior, such as becoming better adapted to feeding on people, might have increased the incidence of bites and thereby of infection. Or shifting human habits might have put an unprecedented number of people in harm's way.

Climate change, too, could have played a part by bringing mosquitoes and people closer together.

Unraveling the mystery and determining its medical relevance requires assessing the evolutionary histories of all three organisms: the human host, as Tishkoff has begun to do; the mosquito; and the malaria parasite itself.

Clues in the genome of the *P. falciparum* microbe suggest a recent, dramatic population expansion. In 1998, Francisco J. Ayala, Steven M. Rich, and two of their colleagues at the University of California, Irvine made a proposal based on their studies of genetic diversity. They suggested that all living *P. falciparum* have descended from a single ancestral strain—a "malarial Eve," as they dubbed it—dating back between 5,750 and 57,500 years.

Such a scenario, called a bottleneck or founding event, usually occurs when a subpopulation of a species branches off and evolves in a new direction. If the new subspecies is more successful than all other populations, it may completely replace them over several generations. This triumph would establish an almost complete genetic homogeneity across the species and thereby reset the species' molecular clock to zero.

Rich and Ayala suggest that just such an ascendant subpopulation of *P. falciparum* arose within the past few thousand to tens of thousands of years. The putative founder could have been a highly adapted parasite that was especially effective at spreading rapidly among people—and particularly deadly, as well.

Since the work of Ayala and Rich, other researchers have probed the genome of *P. falciparum* for the telltale genetic uniformity that indicates a past bottleneck. The preponderance of evidence supports the bottleneck model.

In one study, researchers led by Daniel Hartl, a population geneticist at the Harvard School of Public Health in Boston, examined the DNA in eight geographically diverse populations of *P. falciparum*. Among the specimens, the scientists catalogued the genetic variation found in 25 segments of DNA that don't contain any genes. Such segments are presumed to be unaffected by natural selection.

In the July 20 *Science*, Hartl's group reported little variability in these DNA segments. That uniformity suggests that although distributed from Honduras to Papua New Guinea today, the parasites diverged from a common ancestor at some time within the past 23,000 years, probably less. "Something happened perhaps 6,000 to 10,000 years ago that cleansed the variation that existed in the ancestral population," says Sarah K. Volkman of Harvard University, the paper's lead author.

Other population geneticists have reached a similar conclusion by examining the genes in the parasite's mitochondria. Those structures within cells contain their own DNA, which they pass virtually unaltered from one generation to the next. David J. Conway of the London School of Hygiene and Tropical Medicine, with researchers from five other countries, compared mitochondrial DNA among several strains of *P. falciparum* and one of *Plasmodium reichenowi*, a related parasite that causes malaria in chimpanzees.

In contrast to the extensive variation between *P. falciparum* and *P. reichenowi*, the researchers found little variation in mitochondrial DNA among different strains of *P. falciparum*. If, as earlier data suggest, the two Plasmodium species split 6 to 10 million years ago when chimps and humans diverged, the uniformity of mitochondrial DNA among the *P. falciparum* strains indicates a divergence in recent times. That modern epoch—at most the past 50,000 years, say the researchers—contains the hypothesized bottleneck, they noted in the November 2000 *Molecular And Biochemical Parasitology*.

Mario Coluzzi, a leading mosquito researcher at the University La Sapienza in Rome, argues that *P. falciparum*'s bottleneck could not have occurred by itself, but rather required simultaneous evolution in the mosquito that spreads it. Numerous species and subspecies of mosquitoes serve as carriers, or vectors, for malaria, and some can shuttle multiple species of the parasite between infected people and new hosts.

Most mosquitoes aren't adapted to feed exclusively on people or inhabit their settlements and dwellings, but *Anopheles gambiae* is. As such, it serves as the main vector in Africa for *P. falciparum*.

By living in close association with people in Africa, *A. gambiae* offers the parasite it carries the most reliable promise of rapid transmission to new human hosts. In some regions of Africa, individuals are typically bitten by hundreds of infected mosquitoes per year, says Andrew Spielman, who studies vector-borne diseases at Harvard University's Center for International Development and is a coauthor of *Mosquito* (2001, Hyperion).

Such a continual, rapid cycle of transmission, notes Coluzzi, is essential to *P. falciparum*'s self-perpetuation. The parasite is so destructive that it can't linger long in any one host. He suspects that accelerated transmission unleashed the highly destructive strain of *P. falciparum* that causes the modern scourge.

At one time, conditions were much less favorable to the rapid circulation of *A. gambiae* among people, Coluzzi says. These insects need shallow, sunlit pools of water to lay their eggs in, and the dense forest that covered most of Africa wouldn't have provided such pools. Coluzzi's research suggests *A. gambiae* is highly adaptable, and he argues the mosquito could have fed on other mammals when forest-dwelling people were less accessible.

Rich thinks that under proper conditions, a "super-vector" mosquito could have replaced all contemporary *A. gambiae* while carrying its particular strain of *P. falciparum* along for the ride. He suggests that an extended period of climatic warming around 8,000 years ago might have altered the environment in a way that benefited the super-vector strain.

Agriculture is considered as another factor in malaria's spread. In 1958, anthropologist Frank Livingstone, then a professor at the University of Michigan in Ann Arbor, proposed that ecological changes accompanying the human transition to farming fostered the spread of malaria. That theory puts Africa's first farmers and the land changes they wrought behind the widening sweep of malaria's scythe.

According to Livingstone's scenario, early West African cultivators about 3,000 years ago began clearing forest to grow crops. The change produced two factors favoring *A. gambiae*: more sunlit pools of water in which the insects could breed and a concentrated population of people on which they could feed.

As cultivators slashed, burned, and planted swathes through the forest, *A. gambiae* mosquitoes could have adapted to feed exclusively on people, suggests Coluzzi.

The agricultural scenario is appealing, but the archeological evidence to back it up isn't strong. Slash-and-burn cultivation has been common throughout much of sub-Saharan Africa for at least 500 years, but there is "very scant evidence [of it] in tropical forest zones in the archeological record," says Robert Dewar, an African archeologist at the University of Connecticut in Storrs.

Not all genetic studies in *P. falciparum* support a recent bottleneck, either. Austin L. Hughes, a population geneticist at the University of South Carolina in Columbia, has data showing substantial variation in portions of the parasite's genome that code for certain cell-surface proteins. The host's immune system uses these proteins, called antigens, to identify and attack the parasite. The change of a single molecule, called a point mutation, in the genes that Hughes examined can alter the shape of a surface protein, disguising it from the immune system.

In a study appearing in the Sept. 7 *Proceedings of the Royal Society of London B*, Hughes and Federica Verra, a parasitologist and Coluzzi's colleague in Rome, found a large number of point mutations in 23 locations in the *P. falciparum* genome.

That great variety suggests that *P. falciparum*'s molecular clock has been ticking for at least 300,000 years since its various populations diverged from a common progenitor. In contrast to the bottleneck model, this scenario suggests a relatively stable parasite population as old as modern humans themselves.

Hughes suggests that selective pressure on one or a handful of genes might have eliminated considerable variation along the stretches of DNA that other researchers have studied and it could have given the appearance of a bottleneck.

"The huge amount of antigenic diversity," says Verra, helps the parasite evade the immune system and makes malaria a tricky disease to tackle medically. Immunity after a malaria infection is only partial and impermanent.

Critics of Hughes' report acknowledge the considerable antigenic diversity but doubt that it indicates a long evolutionary period. It could be, Rich says, that the mutations are very ancient and have been maintained over time, even through a bottleneck. Alternatively, he says, they could have developed all of their antigenic diversity in the short time since that bottleneck. "The genes that are the target of vaccine efforts [could be] evolving very, very rapidly," he says.

Rich, who's now at Tufts University Grafton, Mass., and Ayala recently looked at three highly variable *P. falciparum* antigen genes. Much of the variation appears in stretches of DNA characterized by short, repeated sequences of nucleotides and consists of differing numbers of these repeats, they reported in a study published in the June 20, 2000 *Proceedings of the National Academy of Sciences*.

Duplication and deletion of repeat sequences are thought to occur much more quickly than the point mutations that Hughes studied. Thus, Rich and Ayala infer, the high variation found in antigen-coding regions of the *P. falciparum* genome may reflect not an ancient origin but a relentless evolutionary arms race against the human immune system.

Understanding when and how malaria reached epidemic proportions could bear on scientists' plans for developing a vaccine and future therapies. If antigenic diversity stems from the parasite's gradual evolution along with that of people over hundreds of thousands of years, then science may be able to catch up to the parasite and figure out how to shut it down.

If, on the other hand, the antigenic diversity emerged within the last few thousand years, it probably will continue to evolve rapidly in response to the human immune system, drugs, and vaccines. "If a vaccine targets one of those repetitive genes, you're really aiming at a moving target," warns Rich.

Why do disabling or deadly genes sometimes stick around for a long time? Many of the articles you have read demonstrate the power of natural selection to weed out those genes that do not promote survival of the species, so why shouldn't that evolutionary force drive all deleterious, or harmful, alleles out of plant and animal populations? There are many possible responses to these questions, but the basic answer is that natural selection and evolution are far from perfect. For example, some genetic diseases may not become apparent in an organism until well after an organism's reproductive years. By then, he or she may have already passed along "bad" alleles to offspring and future generations. Another simple explanation is that something called "heterozygote advantage" can sometimes maintain a disadvantageous allele in a population because that allele can serve a positive purpose in other respects. Consider sickle-cell anemia: if you inherit two disadvantageous versions of the allele, you are in grave danger

of developing the often fatal blood disease. If you inherit one "good" and one "bad" form, you may be more likely to stay healthy than friends with two "good" genes. That is because people heterozygous for sickle-cell anemia are actually more resistant to malaria, a some-times-deadly parasitic infection. Ashkenazi Jews suffer from a slew of genetic diseases that are relatively rare in the rest of the population, and researchers have long assumed that many Ashkenazi diseases were the result of a system similar to sickle-cell anemia. New research suggests the genetic and evolutionary mecha-nisms at work in certain diseases common to the Ashkenazi may in fact be quite different than those of sickle-cell anemia. Yet they still provide a compelling example of evolutionary forces at work. —KH

"Stanford Research Points to Chance as Cause of Genetic Diseases in Ashkenazi Jews"
by Stanford University Medical Center
February 27, 2003

A population of Jewish people known as the Ashkenazi Jews have an unusually high risk of several genetic diseases, and up until now, no one has understood why. Was it random chance that made mutations so common or did evolution play a role in keeping mutations around?

The answer to this question, said researchers at Stanford University Medical Center, appears to be chance. Their findings appear in the March online issue of the American Journal of Human Genetics and in the journal's April print edition.

Some disease mutations unusually common in Ashkenazi Jews, who make up 90 percent of the American Jewish population, include Tay-Sachs disease and some forms of breast cancer, high cholesterol and hemophilia. Four of these disorders, including Tay-Sachs disease, are in a class of diseases called lysosomal storage diseases. People with these disorders lack enzymes that break down toxins into harmless compounds. Instead, the toxins are stored in cellular compartments called lysosomes, where they can build up to high levels and eventually damage the cell.

"It's been known for a long time that Ashkenazi Jews have a high risk of these lysosomal storage diseases," said Neil Risch, PhD, professor of genetics, statistics, and health research and policy at the School of Medicine and one of the senior authors on the study. "The majority opinion has been that there must be some selective advantage for those mutations."

Researchers had suspected that lysosomal storage diseases may be similar to sickle cell anemia, in which people who carry two mutated copies of the gene have a disease, but those who inherit one copy of the mutation are protected against malaria. Those people—called carriers—are more likely to be healthy, have more children and pass their mutation on to future generations.

If carriers of lysosomal storage mutations were protected against other diseases, then those mutations should be more common in Ashkenazi Jewish populations than mutations that cause diseases unrelated to lysosomal storage. Risch and his colleagues analyzed DNA sequences from Ashkenazi Jewish people and compared how common mutations were in lysosomal storage disease genes vs. other disease genes.

The researchers found that mutations in lysosomal storage disease genes are no more common than mutations that cause other inherited diseases in the Ashkenazi Jewish population. This suggests that carriers for lysosomal storage mutations had no benefit over their peers. Instead, Risch said, these mutations were probably present in the Jews who coalesced into the Ashkenazi Jewish population 900 years ago.

"The mutations that persisted represent whatever the people who had the most children happened to be carrying," Risch said. It just happened that those who founded the Ashkenazi Jewish population had disease mutations and passed them along to their children. Because Ashkenazi Jews tend to marry within their own population, those mutations remained common.

Risch also looked at the regional distribution of mutations in Ashkenazi Jews, and the age of those mutations. He found three points in time when mutations entered the population. One mutation has been in the Jewish population for 120 generations—around the time that the Jewish people formed a distinct population in the Middle East. This mutation causes a type of hemophilia called Factor 11 deficiency type II.

The majority of the mutations—including all of the mutations in lysosomal storage genes—entered the population when the Ashkenazi Jews formed a coherent group about 50 generations ago. The final mutations cropped up in the Lithuanian Ashkenazi Jews about 12 generations ago.

Reprinted with permission from Stanford School of Medicine Office of Communication and Publication and Amy Adams.

Necessity truly is the mother of invention. Sometimes, the desperate need for a new technology speeds its development. For centuries, diabetes killed many of its sufferers. Then, in 1920, Canadian doctor Frederick Banting and his colleagues discovered insulin, finally offering diabetics some hope in controlling the disease and leading longer, healthier lives. Other times, the technology comes first, and unexpected uses for it emerge later. In the Human Genome Project, a competitive race to sequence the entire human genome, researchers developed sophisticated techniques to sequence long stretches of DNA quickly. The main intent of this project was to identify all of approximately 30,000 human genes. The project was successfully completed in 2003, and the resulting DNA map has proven to be of enormous value to a wide range of researchers. When the deadly illness SARS (severe acute respiratory syndrome) emerged as

a worldwide epidemic in 2003, Chinese and American researchers collaborated to identify and fight the virus. They used techniques honed during the Human Genome Project to pinpoint the genetic changes that led the virus to evolve into a more deadly agent and to trace the virus's possible origin in civet cats. The SARS epidemic proves once again that to understand disease and epidemiology, you also need to understand evolution. —KH

"New Genetic Techniques Show Deadly Evolution of SARS Virus"
by Peter Gorner
Chicago Tribune, January 30, 2004

Powerful new genetic techniques have enabled Chinese scientists to track the DNA fingerprints of the SARS virus as it jumped from animals to people and evolved with unparalleled speed—taking only a few months to turn deadly and spread around the world.

By pinpointing the genetic mutations that occurred in the coronavirus that causes SARS, the research points the way to strategies for developing vaccines and treatments for SARS and other viral diseases.

It also marks the first time that gene-sequencing techniques derived from the Human Genome Project were used against a new epidemic, and it bolsters the evidence for the specific animal origins of SARS, scientists said.

The research, published in this week's edition of the journal *Science*, examined viral samples from infected animals and humans. It indicates that the virus tried and rejected many guises as it grew deadlier and more infectious.

In the early cases in China, for example, only about 3 percent of people in direct contact with infected patients developed severe acute respiratory syndrome. Within a few months, however, the infection rate from direct contact rose to nearly 70 percent.

"This is a very disturbing process to watch. We see the virus fine-tuning itself to enhance its access to a new host—humans," said the study's co-lead author, Chung-I Wu, chairman of ecology and evolution at the University of Chicago. Wu and his team analyzed the findings collected from scientists in China.

"As the virus improves itself, it learns how to spread from person to person. Then it sticks with the version that is most effective and we have an epidemic," said Wu, a leading expert in the evolution of genes.

The findings underline the importance of early recognition and control of outbreaks of emerging infectious diseases before they get out of hand.

Highly contagious, SARS causes pneumonia, high fever, headaches, body aches, diarrhea and other symptoms. It is fatal in about 10 percent of cases. Blamed on a new coronavirus, called SARS-associated coronavirus, the infection is spread by droplets produced when an infected person coughs or sneezes.

Once the virus adapted to the human environment, SARS became stable and widespread, causing a panic between March and May before being contained by intensive medical care, quarantine, isolation, the tracing of infected people's contacts and other public health measures.

According to Guo-Ping Zhao and colleagues at the Chinese SARS Molecular Epidemiology Consortium, two genotypes dominated the early phase of the epidemic. Both differed from later viral samples by having deletions in DNA in a region known as Orf8.

This early phase was characterized by rapid mutations at specific "hot spots" along the viral genome, the researchers found. Those mutations caused gene changes, which in turn altered amino acids in what is known as a "spike protein" that the virus needs to adhere to host cells.

A Link to Wild Animals

The scientists analyzed 11 early cases that seemingly developed independently in different locations in the Pearl River Delta area of Guangdong Province, China.

In this region, they wrote, rapid economic development has led to "culinary habits involving exotic animals." Six of the 11 early cases of SARS involved contact with wild animals.

The same strains that researchers found in those early cases also were found in farmed civet cats, a Chinese delicacy. It is not known if humans caught the infection from them or from some other mammal, but civets were banned from importation into the U.S. earlier this month.

"We suspect the jumping [of the virus] from the cat into humans probably occurred in late October or early November of 2002," Wu said.

He said he doesn't know how this leap occurred. "We can time the jump, but we don't know the mechanism," he said. "I suppose if an infected cat sneezed, you could catch it, just as you can catch influenza from the sneeze of another person."

But other experts said the cat connection remains unproved.

"It's premature to say civets were the source," said Dr. Mark Denison, a coronavirus specialist at Vanderbilt University. "Nobody has proved civets are a reservoir for SARS. We can say other civets had the same virus, or that a virus like the civet virus got into humans and then underwent additional changes.

"Nonetheless, I am very impressed by this study," Denison said. "We're seeing a new tool that will be rapidly used with any emerging threat, like avian flu, from different places in different patients."

Big Outbreak Slows Changes

When looking at the early-stage viruses, the Chinese researchers discovered a series of genetic motifs that enabled them to distinguish between different virus lineages.

They also found that the virus' gene substitution rate slowed during "super-spreader" events, such as the major SARS outbreak in a hospital in Guangzhou that started on Jan. 31, 2003. This outbreak produced 130 cases, 106 of which were acquired in the hospital.

A doctor from that hospital carried the virus to a hotel in Hong Kong on Feb. 21, infecting other guests, who carried the virus to Vietnam, Canada, Singapore and the U.S., the scientists said.

One predominant genotype finally arose during the last phase.

"That's the one that caused the panic between March and May," Wu said.

Before the viral outbreak was quelled, SARS had spread to clusters of infected patients in more than two dozen countries in North and South America, Europe and Asia. The virus had sickened more than 8,000 people worldwide. It killed nearly 800 people and caused considerable fear and billions of dollars in tourism losses.

The U.S. reported 192 probable and suspect cases, only eight of which were confirmed as the SARS coronavirus. All the patients recovered.

"The new work dramatically illustrates the new tools we have for getting a grip on emerging viruses," said Richard Gibbs, director of the Human Genome Sequencing Center at Baylor University.

"If you look at HIV, it took quite a while for genetic analysis to contribute strongly to the story [in terms of new drugs]. Here, straightaway, the SARS virus emerges and the techniques are right there waiting for it."

When climate experts began making maps to illustrate how global climate change might affect certain parts of the world, biologists began overlaying those maps with others showing species' ranges. Then they got worried. The maps indicated that the continued existence of many species would be threatened by global warming. Classic sugar maples of the northeastern United States, for example, simply cannot survive in a warmer world. If climate change happens as quickly as many suspect it will, the maples will not be able to spread seeds quickly enough to follow cooler weather north. In general, evolution is a slow process. It is rare to see any substantial change in a species over several dozen generations. So perhaps we should not be surprised that, as humans radically alter the global environment, evolved animal behaviors that adapt to these new conditions cannot always keep up. In fact, as Lila Guterman points out in this article, organisms often stubbornly stick to behaviors evolution has taught them over thousands of years but which are suddenly no longer applicable to their surroundings. Sometimes these behaviors will actually prove harmful—even fatal—in a world radically altered by human intervention. For this reason, we are beginning to see beetles attempting to mate with brown beer bottles—and dying for their error. Similarly, sea turtles are ingesting— and being asphyxiated by—plastic bags, mistakenly believing them to be jellyfish. —KH

"Trapped by Evolution: Animals' Instincts Lead Them Astray in Modern, Much-Altered Environments"
by Lila Guterman
Chronicle of Higher Education, October 18, 2002

Pity the male buprestid beetle. Evolution taught him a lesson that, until only recently, served him well: Go out and mate with a brown, shiny object that has small bumps like the ones covering your own wings. That is a female of the species.

Unfortunately, some beer bottles exhibit the same characteristics.

Scientists discovered nearly 20 years ago that the two-inch-long male *Julodimorpha bakewelli* beetles in Australia are fooled by stray bottles and try to inseminate them. In some instances, the mistake means not only sexual frustration but also death: Ants attack the beetle as he mounts the bottle, an act he won't interrupt even as his genitals are bitten.

In a paper in this month's *Trends in Ecology & Evolution*, three ecologists say the beetle's behavior is just one example of a common, but underappreciated, phenomenon. When humans alter the environment, they often cause problems more subtle than simply destroying habitat, the researchers argue. The changes can create a situation in which an animal's evolved behavior hurts its chances of surviving or reproducing, which in turn can send the species downhill, and fast.

"If you're dealing with a population that's in serious trouble, this is something you ought to consider," says Paul W. Sherman, a professor of animal behavior at Cornell University, who is one of the authors of the paper. "Evolved behaviors are there for adaptive reasons. If we [disrupt] the normal environment, we can drive a population right to extinction."

The Wrong Cue

Mr. Sherman and his two colleagues call the mechanism an "evolutionary trap." Their new term expands on the concept of the ecological trap, which describes why species bypass better habitats to live in less suitable ones. Animals go to those poorer sites because they are led astray by environmental cues that no longer help in an environment altered by humans.

More than 20 years ago, two ecologists described an ecological trap that appears in forests fragmented into patches by activities like logging, road-building, agriculture, and development. Birds from 21 species were putting nests near forest edges, even though predators frequently ate their eggs and their nestlings there. The researchers suggested that the birds had evolved to prefer sites with a variety of vegetation types because, in the past, that had meant better foraging and good protection against predators. But the cue—heterogeneous plant life—no longer indicated a better habitat, because fragmentation had produced more forest edges with such a variety, and an accompanying surge in the number of predators there.

Scientists have discovered many other ecological traps since then. For example, some grassland birds choose to nest in pastures, based on an evolutionary preference for low vegetation. But when the pastures are mown, young chicks are unable to fly away to escape. Mammals, too, fall into ecological traps. In the past 50 years, manatees have been found farther north in Florida's waters, because of warm water discharged from power plants. But whenever a plant is turned off, for maintenance or other reasons, the manatees encounter water too cold for them.

The concept of ecological traps has always applied to habitat choice. But now Mr. Sherman, Martin A. Schlaepfer, and Michael C. Runge point out that changes in the environment can cause formerly positive behavior to be harmful in other ways, interfering with breeding, migration, and feeding, for example.

Mr. Sherman began thinking about that broader possibility when he was studying wood ducks. Normally the ducks, *Aix sponsa*, nest in cavities of dead trees, laying 10 to 12 eggs at a time. For about 50 years, wildlife managers have erected nesting boxes for wood ducks to help them reproduce. Strangely, though, the boxes often caused more harm than good.

The Cornell professor studied the birds for about 15 years to figure out why. Female wood ducks have adapted to a dearth of appropriate nest sites by trying to follow other ducks to their nest cavities to lay an egg or two there, or even take over the cavity. The nesting boxes were simply too conspicuous—ducks were laying 30 to 50 eggs in a single box. That's too many eggs for one duck to incubate; many nests were then abandoned.

Making the boxes easy to find was an attempt to assist the ducks, Mr. Sherman says. But it also helped female ducks to locate others' nests rather than find their own. "The solution is a real simple one," he says. "Hide the boxes back in the woods."

Mr. Sherman also saw hints of a trap in the behavior of a rodent that has "just about winked out from the earth," in the words of Mr. Runge, an ecologist at the U.S. Geological Service's Patuxent Wildlife Research Center, in Maryland. Perhaps as few as 350 individuals remain of the northern Idaho ground squirrel, *Spermophilus brunneus brunneus.* Mr. Sherman has studied one population in Adams County, Idaho, where from 1987 to 1999 the squirrels' numbers declined from 272 to 10. He and other scientists wanted to know why.

The answer may be as simple as not having enough food. The squirrels' habitat has been transformed because people have prevented fires from occurring, allowing pine trees to invade what used to be open meadows. Shrubs have elbowed out the grasses and herbs that the squirrels feed on.

But Mr. Sherman and Mr. Runge thought more might be going on. The small, short-tailed squirrels hibernate for eight months of the year. During the late spring and summer, they must eat enough to triple their body weight to survive the winter. They also must reproduce—or not even try.

Though this behavior has never been studied in northern Idaho ground squirrels, a close relative's reproductive efforts each spring are dictated by how much food is available. "That's a very smart evolutionary adaptation," says Mr. Runge. "Why have pups when you know you're not going to be able to feed them?"

He and Mr. Sherman speculate in a paper due to appear in *Ecology* that the squirrels may be fooled by the greenery present in the altered habitat when they emerge from hibernation. Expecting food throughout the summer, they invest energy in mating. But not enough food becomes available late in the summer for them to fatten up sufficiently. "The animals have gone ahead and reproduced and put themselves in jeopardy, but there's no payback, and they starve over the winter," says Mr. Sherman.

Though it hasn't been proved, the idea of an evolutionary trap threatening the squirrels is intriguing, says Eric Yensen, a professor of biology at Albertson College, in Caldwell, Idaho, who also studies the northern Idaho ground squirrel. "It gives us some things we can test . . . Somebody's going to have to do a behavioral study to figure out just what they're cueing on."

In the meantime, because of limited funds and the desperately small squirrel populations, wildlife managers with Idaho's Department of Fish and Game and the U.S. Forest Service have begun prescribed burns and supplemental feeding to try to save the rodents without fully understanding what is threatening them. Bruce A. Haak, a state biologist, says some of the populations are already rebounding.

Wayward Lizards

While Mr. Sherman and Mr. Runge contemplated trapped squirrels, Mr. Schlaepfer, then a graduate student in natural resources at Cornell and now a postdoctoral fellow there, was thousands of miles away in Costa Rica, thinking along the same lines about reptiles. He was studying the lizard *Norops polylepis*, which normally lives in cool, shady areas. But the lizards had been found laying eggs in pastures that people had cleared in the forest.

The problem, he found, is that the adults do not survive well in the pastures. He has not figured out why.

"These lizards may never have seen a pasture in their evolutionary past," Mr. Schlaepfer says. He wondered if they had evolved to lay eggs in the sunniest areas of the forest, since those were the warmest. "They might be drawn to pastures in search of good egg-laying sites, unaware that the adults were going to be hammered."

Back in Ithaca, Mr. Sherman was serving on Mr. Schlaepfer's dissertation committee. They discovered that they and Mr. Runge had all been thinking about how animals get trapped by their adaptive behaviors when they are in human-influenced environments.

When Mr. Schlaepfer started looking for examples of other evolutionary traps described in the scientific literature, he found numerous cases. In the mid-'90s, sea-turtle hatchlings born on Florida beaches were dying because, after emerging from their eggs, they turned inland instead of heading out to sea. Scientists discovered that hatchlings normally rely on light on the horizon over the ocean to decide which direction to migrate. But the light from nearby homes and hotels was fooling them. Florida has protected the turtles by requiring building owners either to use light of a different wavelength or to shield the lights from the beach.

Other examples came up: Because of global warming, the insects that are fed on by great tits—small, yellow-and-black birds found in Europe—appear earlier in the season than they used to. But length of daylight, not temperature, determines when the birds lay their eggs. So the young hatch after the bulk of their food has come and gone. Leatherback turtles sometimes eat plastic bags, presumably because of their similarity in appearance to a favorite food, jellyfish.

Mr. Runge says that all four animals he's currently studying—manatees, grassland birds, pintail ducks, and the ground squirrels—may be stuck in evolutionary traps. "It's just a coincidence that they're all facing this. Or maybe it's not. It could be a ubiquitous mechanism."

Hanna Kokko, an assistant professor of ecology at the University of Jyväskylä, in Finland, has done theoretical work on ecological traps. She suspects that evolutionary traps, too, are probably very common. "I would expect that now there is a name for this phenomenon, we might pay a lot more attention and find a lot more," she says.

Finding the problem sometimes gets you most of the way toward solving it, as was the case with the sea turtles and the wood ducks. But too often, conservation biologists and wildlife managers don't look to behavior for causes of population declines, say Mr. Sherman and his colleagues.

"If we hear about a declining population, the typical response is: We've got to buy more of its habitat and save the habitat it's living in," he says. "With the wood ducks, we could have bought lots more habitat and put out more nesting boxes, but that wouldn't have solved the problem."

At first glance, the following article relates a simple story about conservation and the dangers of overbreeding. The claim: the agricultural industry and market forces are destroying the genetic diversity of American livestock. Where once we had dozens of types of milk cows, Holsteins now represent more than 90 percent of the industry's dairy stock. Yet there are also two key evolutionary issues at stake here. First, the dwindling genetic diversity of livestock illustrates how people can be a selective force in evolution, operating in much the same way as natural selection. Selective breeding of plants and pets for certain characteristics has created genetically

distinct feed corn and sweet corn, dalmatians and dachshunds, for example. The second evolutionary issue raised by this article is that diversity is important. Phenotypic and genetic diversity do not just create a pleasing visual variety in living things. They also give organisms the ability to respond to changing circumstances and, therefore, survive as a species in the future. The ability of genetically diverse livestock and plants to adapt and survive may help humans survive, too. In the mid-1800s, for example, a potato blight resulted in deaths by famine of more than a million Irish peasants. Many biologists argue that a lack of genetic diversity among potatoes left the entire crop vulnerable to the blight. Had there been different strains, some potato varieties would almost surely have been resistant to the disease. —KH

"Dying Breeds: Livestock Are Developing a Largely Unrecognized Biodiversity Crisis"
by Janet Raloff
Science News, October 4, 1997

When it comes to milk production, nothing beats Holsteins. For the farmer who takes care to keep them cool, sated with high-energy chow, and milked regularly—often under the management of a sophisticated computer—these familiar black-and-white cows produce an average of 2,275 gallons of milk each per year. The average Brown Swiss, in contrast, produced only 1,820 gallons last year, and a Jersey less than 1,600.

The Holstein's milk generation has become so legendary that the roughly 9.2 million of them in the United States now represent an estimated 91 percent of the nation's dairy stock. Not surprisingly, Holsteins have achieved almost as daunting a dominance of dairying in many other Western nations, notes Richard H.L. Lutwyche of the Rare Breeds Survival Trust in Stoneleigh Park, England.

However, what's good for the individual farmer may not reflect what's in the best long-term interest of the animals or even dairying, argues H. Peter Jorgensen, a founder and former director of the Institute for Agricultural Biodiversity at Luther College in Decorah, Iowa. The focus on a single breed is eroding the bovine gene pool, he argues, creating increasingly clonelike generations of all too genetically similar animals.

Were a disease to develop for which Holsteins carried some particular inherited susceptibility, U.S. milk production could crash. Or if faltering economic conditions made low-tech, grass-fed dairying the only affordable approach, farmers might again want animals that can produce a lot of milk without coddling. Kerrys, Dutch Belted, and Milking Devons may carry genes for some of these traits. However, being among the world's rarest dairy breeds, their ability to supply such features would disappear if they were allowed to die off.

Dairy cows aren't the only livestock whose genetic diversity is waning rapidly. Of 15 breeds of swine raised in this country just 50 years ago, 8 are now extinct and most of the remaining purebred types are seriously imperiled, according to the American Livestock Breeds Conservancy (ALBC) in Pittsboro, N.C. The organization's most recent North American livestock census identifies hosts of other once-popular horses, goats, sheep, and asses poised on the brink of extinction.

Worldwide, at least 1,500 of the roughly 5,000 domesticated livestock breeds "are now rare—represented by less than 20 breeding males on the planet or less than 1,000 breeding females," explains Keith Hammond, senior officer for Animal Genetic Resources with the United Nations Food and Agriculture Organization (FAO) in Rome.

For the past decade, his department has been coordinating surveys and status reports on livestock breeds in FAO's 180 member nations. Its latest data suggest that 5 percent of those highly endangered breeds disappear from the face of the Earth annually—which, Hammond notes, comes to an average of more than one a week.

Overall, he told *Science News*, "a larger proportion of genetic resources is in danger [of extinction] in the animal sector than in any other area of agrobiodiversity."

All domesticated livestock today belong to one of some 80 species. However, only about 14 of these play an important role in food and agriculture.

Farmers have worked with these animals over the centuries to develop highly specialized breeds that embody distinct combinations of traits. The French alone developed 200 different breeds of cattle during the 18th and 19th centuries within the two domesticated bovine species, Jorgensen notes, and the British developed 40 different breeds of sheep.

From arid regions have emerged hardy cows able to weather heat and drought. Siberia produced a breed of cattle that tolerates winter temperatures as low as $-60\,^{\circ}$C ($-76\,^{\circ}$F). Elsewhere, breeds have arisen with especially strong resistance to disease and parasites, superior mothering qualities, prodigious strength for draft applications, or a tendency to lay down predominantly lean tissue.

However, since World War II, agriculture has been undergoing a transformation—moving from a family enterprise to big business. This change, which the ALBC describes as industrialization, has had a profound effect on which breeds remain popular.

Farmers once had perhaps 30 cows, each of which had a name. Today's herds typically number hundreds and sometimes thousands of nameless animals. Accompanying the change in scale has been the introduction of technology to gauge production efficiency.

"When my dad was farming," Jorgensen recalls, "he would put a scoop of feed in front of each cow and hay in the manger. We didn't have the technology to precisely measure what went in and out of each animal," a requirement for quantitative comparisons of breeds. Today, as cows enter stalls in the dairy barn, a sensor identifies each individual from the computer chip in her ear. Then software analyzes the cow's recent milking performance and triggers a feed dispenser to meter out precisely how much she will need.

Robert Hawes traces the dawn of a similar revolution in chicken husbandry to competitive egg-laying tests that the Agriculture Department began offering in the 1920s. The compelling results convinced farmers that they could reliably expect more eggs—and money— from particular breeds, says Hawes, a poultry expert at the University of Maine in Orono.

Before long, many of the more than 60 breeds that had been raised in the United States were abandoned in favor of just a handful of high performers. Today, Hawes says, five breeds supply almost all of the chicken meat and brown eggs sold as food. White eggs now come almost exclusively from a single breed, white leghorns.

Though bird fanciers still raise other species, Hawes says their emphasis is on producing pretty chickens, often at the expense of utilitarian traits, such as an ability to lay many eggs or eggs with firm shells.

Swine and several other species are losing genetic diversity in response to another trend: crossbreeding.

Though virtually all purebred swine are pigmented and sport bristly hair, most children picture the pig only as the pink movie star Babe. Such unpigmented and frequently hairless pigs—which usually result from a crossing of several different breeds—constitute the majority of pigs raised in the United States and Britain, notes Lutwyche.

Promoted by vertically integrated hog operations— industrial firms that not only mass-rear hogs but also slaughter them and package the meat for supermarkets—these pigs have been bred to bulk up quickly on a high-protein diet, laying down fairly lean meat. In Britain, Lutwyche notes, any pig that doesn't match this profile encounters "enormous bigotry by the butchery trade and supermarkets," which have argued that the public "won't buy meat from a pigmented animal."

So effective has their lobbying been, he says, that Britain's Meat and Livestock Commission has devalued such meat. "Now, even when farmers bring in the most perfect carcass," he told *Science News*, "they're immediately docked 25 pence a kilo [18 cents per pound], if it came from a [pigmented] pig."

Increasingly, these industrialized livestock operations are also wresting control of livestock genetics from those who raise the animals, points out ALBC's Carolyn J. Christman. For instance, ever fewer farmers raising pigs, turkeys, and chickens mate animals but instead are acquiring them from breeding facilities.

Just four or five companies control all the genetic stocks for commercially reared broiler chickens in North America and Europe. "If these folks are accountants and don't know much about biology or are looking for the short-term gain," she says, "they can quickly throw away a large share of the animals' genetic variability."

This business approach to livestock management is also compartmentalizing what had once been multipurpose breeds into distinct functional niches. For instance, while Holsteins rule the dairy world, they are nonplayers in the premium U.S. beef market, where Angus, Herefords, and Simmentals reign.

Optimizing for a niche, Lutwyche argues, "leaves no room for breeds like the Longhorn or Gloucester cattle—those all-purpose breeds that are neither the heaviest milkers nor animals with the preferred beef conformation [ratios of lean to fat and of meat to bone]."

Hoping to slow the genetic erosion that accompanies any loss of livestock varieties, several organizations have begun working to conserve the so-called heritage breeds through a broad range of programs. The Rare Breeds Survival Trust, for instance, has begun accrediting butchers who offer meat from pure heritage breeds. This awarding of what amounts to its seal of approval, Lutwyche says, "is proving extremely successful in helping rescue certain sheep, cattle, and pigs."

His group has also publicized data showing that meat from certain "very primitive" sheep—such as the Hebridean, Soay, and Manx Loughtan—contains very little cholesterol and an usually high ratio of polyunsaturated to saturated fats. This has permitted farmers who raise such breeds to develop health-conscious specialty markets for their meat.

The Institute for Agricultural Biodiversity has taken a different tack. In 1992, it purchased 10 mulefoot hogs, the most endangered U.S. swine, and placed small breeding groups of them in foster care with livestock farmers. Today, those animals, now numbering around 50, represent about half of the once-popular breed's global population.

Safeguard for Agricultural Varieties in Europe (SAVE), a group based in Germany, has been active in coordinating a number of similar projects in war-torn and economically ravaged areas of Eastern Europe. One of its projects involves the Turopolje pigs of Croatia. While remaining under their owner's loose control, these hardy, free-ranging swine normally spend 10 months a year in meadows and forests.

The breed was already severely endangered when civil war swept through the pig's native range 6 years ago. None of these animals would likely have survived the war without some outside intervention, says Hans-Peter Grunenfelder of SAVE's St. Gallen, Switzerland, office. His organization lobbied the Croatian government to provide about $120 per sow to help defray the extra costs incurred as farmers were instructed to move their pigs into barns for year-round feeding and protection from poachers.

Three years ago, SAVE also collected three young boars and three sows to begin a breeding program at the Zagreb Zoo. As hostilities worsened, these animals were eventually evacuated to Vienna. Today, as a first step toward the management of Turopolje breeding to preserve what genetic diversity remains, SAVE is coordinating efforts for DNA testing of the 40 or so pigs known to remain.

Heroic as SAVE's efforts are, most of them take place out of the public eye. To build an appreciation for what the world risks losing, it helps to have representatives of these animals firmly in view, says Elaine Shirley, a livestock conservator at the Colonial Williamsburg (Va.) Foundation, the nation's oldest and largest outdoor living-history museum.

The 173-acre center, which preserves—and recreates through activities—pre-Revolutionary America, has long made livestock a part of its programs. But for years, there had been no effort to use breeds that had been raised during the colonial period. For instance, "the sheep we had were basically a crossbreed that looked like sheep in paintings and drawings of the 18th century," Shirley says. "While they had the right look, heaven knows what their [genetic constitution] was."

Fifteen years ago, she says, a decision was made to begin raising authentic 18th century breeds. "And while we're at it, we decided, let's work with the animals that need the most help." Within 3 years, their first heritage breeds arrived—extremely endangered Leicester Long-wool sheep and Milking Devons (which have died out in Great Britain but number about 150 throughout North America). Since then, they've added some chickens, and they plan to acquire appropriate horses.

Unlike farmers, who may be best suited to raising these animals, Shirley says, museums and zoos have enough time and resources to educate the public about the growing rarity of such breeds and about the potentially valuable genetic resources they carry. In fact, ALBC observes, agriculture's "unwanted breeds" increasingly hold much of the genetic diversity in livestock. As such, "their conservation is an insurance policy necessary for agriculture to face the challenges of an unknown future."

While Jorgensen agrees, he would argue that they should be conserved as more than an insurance policy. "They are just as important a historical artifact as any movies, paintings, or Frank Lloyd Wright house that we go to great expense to preserve. As living artifacts of the greatest agriculture in the world, they deserve at least some little corner where they can be appreciated by our descendants."

One fascinating aspect of evolutionary theory is how easy it is to apply it to other disciplines and different systems of study. For example, experimental computer scientists are drawing on the power of natural selection to generate highly effective programming. They simply craft a few quick-and-dirty programs to perform a certain job and then add some random "mutations" that occasionally alter the programs. The programs whose alterations allow them to perform the job more effectively or efficiently are rewarded by the programmers with the ability to reproduce themselves, thus replicating the basic processes of evolution. Now consider linguistics, the study of world languages and the relationships between them. In recent years, linguists have co-opted analysis programs developed by evolutionary biologists to uncover genetic relationships among organisms. It is a general truism in evolutionary biology that the greater the differences found in a suite of important genes, the more distantly related are the organisms. Linguists are finding that the same can be said, in general, about languages: a greater difference in words between two languages indicates that the languages split away from each other at a more distant time in history. However, some scientists and linguists argue over whether it is appropriate to treat *words like genes. Word use is inherited culturally, if not genetically, but words are shared between languages, whereas genes cannot be swapped. The research projects described in the following article are fascinating attempts to establish the validity of an evolutionary approach to linguistics. More basically, they seek to answer the very same, age-old questions posed by evolutionary biologists—who are we, where do we come from, when did we come from there, and how did we get here? —KH*

"Searching for the Tree of Babel: Linguistic Evolution May Shed Light on History"
by John Pickrell
Science News, May 25, 2002

A picture is generally valued at 1,000 words. What might be the worth of an image of the 7,000 or so languages now spoken in the world? Scientists searching for patterns within this cacophony of lingoes are convinced that languages hold pivotal clues to questions about human history that other areas of study have been unable to answer. In their quest to demonstrate this new idea, these scientists are finding themselves in stiff debate with others who argue that the approach amounts to barking up the wrong tree.

The controversial approach treats languages as though they were biological species and applies analytical methods developed by evolutionary biologists. Although linguists previously have created trees of languages, they haven't used computational methods to rapidly reconstruct relationships between large groups of languages.

Anthropologists and other investigators are using their new, more extensive language trees to trace the historical relationships of different cultural groups, from people conversing in Gujarati and Hindi to those speaking Navajo and Quecha. These researchers claim that, with that information in hand, questions about migration patterns, agriculture, and other society-changing practices become answerable in new ways.

Language trees are useful for depicting relationships of communities in the past 5,000 to 10,000 years or so, a period too short to be resolved by genetics—and exactly the time for which anthropologists and archeologists are seeking new streams of data.

Linguistic Species

When biologists build family trees among species, they look for shared characters—such as the vertebrate spine—or specific genetic sequences. Species with the greatest similarities are grouped to create a tree branch with several extensions. Then, those branches that share the most characters are put together into a bough. This tree of hierarchical relationships, known as a phylogeny, traces a path from ancestral species at the trunk to the most recently evolved species out on the twigs.

Charles Darwin alluded to the notion that languages evolve and diverge as species do. Like genetic systems, which are made up of nucleotides, genes, and individuals, says Mark Pagel, an evolutionary biologist at the University of Reading in England, languages have discrete units: letters, syllables, and words. Language, like a set of genes, is generally transmitted from parents to offspring. And just as mutations in DNA provide the basic biological variations on which natural selection thrives, changes also occur in languages. Variations in pronunciation or meaning are either rejected or preserved in the transfer of language from parents to their children.

Though natural selection per se doesn't act on new word variants, a form of cultural selection certainly does, says Pagel. For example, a catchier version of a word, such as aeroplane rather than flying machine, is more likely to persist.

For many decades, linguists used a tree approach, says Pagel. Comparisons, however, had generally been limited to a small number of languages, and the language analysts didn't take advantage of computer-based quantitative methods.

Russell Gray, an evolutionary biologist at the University of Auckland in New Zealand, notes that for as few as 10 languages, there are an astonishing 34 million possible trees that can be drawn. "For over 100 languages, you're talking about more possible trees than there are atoms in the universe," he adds. Now, Gray says, it's becoming possible to churn out trees for very large data sets.

"These methods are entirely appropriate," concurs Colin Renfrew, an archaeologist at the University of Cambridge in England. "Given that historical linguistics uses many discrete pieces of information, quantitative and technical methods of this sort are long overdue."

To test the mettle of the language-tree approach, researchers have been building hierarchies for Pacific islanders, sub-Saharan Africans, and Eurasians from Iceland to Bangladesh.

Branching Bantu

Clare Janaki Holden, an anthropologist at University College London in England, has used the phylogenetic method to produce a tree of 75 Bantu languages, which are spoken in the southern half of Africa.

Holden set out to examine whether a language tree might reflect the broader cultural history of the region, specifically the spread of farming. This is a good test of the approach, she says, since scientists using archaeological methods have already outlined the diffusion of agriculture in the region.

Holden used a preexisting data set of 92 words of basic vocabulary found in all 75 languages. These are words, such as man or hand, that are essential in all languages. Such words are thought to evolve slowly and be unique to a language.

The data were analyzed with computing software that groups languages so that those sharing the most words are deemed the most closely related. The tree that this effort produced largely agreed with previous linguistic work, says Holden. One difference was that a group of East African languages appeared in her tree closely related to some found in more southerly areas.

Holden and her colleagues at University College are now using linguistic trees to test theories about cultural traits. By mapping traits, such as farming or marriage practices, onto language trees, these researchers can find out how many times a practice evolved and whether it might be correlated with other genetic or cultural factors.

In research chronicled in the April 22 *Proceedings of the Royal Society of London B*, Holden compares the evolutionary scenarios suggested by her language trees with published archeological scenarios for the spread of farming in Africa from 5,000 to 1,500 years ago. The archaeological record suggests major African migrations of farmers. The first was a southerly spread of Neolithic crop farmers from western Africa into central-African forests. In the second mass migration, cattle farmers streamed south from Lake Victoria in eastern Africa.

Each of the two major language groupings in Holden's tree is spoken in areas inhabited by descendants of people who followed one of these two migrations. The languages "mirror closely the spread of farming for both these western and eastern streams," says Holden.

Pacific Diaspora

On the opposite side of the planet, in Auckland, Gray has been using similar methods to produce an Austronesian language tree. This group comprises about 1,000 languages spoken by 270 million people across the Pacific. Gray and his coworker Fiona Jordan, an anthropologist now at University College London, are using their tree to test hypotheses about the timing and sequence of colonization in the Pacific islands.

The researchers created a tree via a process similar to that of Holden. However, the data set—5,185 words from 77 Austronesian languages—was not confined to basic vocabulary.

"What we found was very congruent with how most linguists would group the languages," says Jordan. A few languages from close-in islands, however, did appear grouped with languages spoken on islands much farther out in the Pacific. This may be due to lingual complexities created by terms absorbed from other languages, says Jordan.

Jordan and Gray have considered a hypothesis, supported by archaeological evidence, regarding the colonization of Pacific islands. Around 6,000 years ago, farmers from Taiwan and southern China may have migrated 10,000 miles over water from Taiwan to western Polynesia in just 2,100 years. Known as "the express train to Polynesia," this controversial idea was proposed in 1988 by Jared Diamond of the University of California, Los Angeles School of Medicine.

Gray and Jordan tested the scenario. If the theory is correct, says Jordan, languages found nearest to mainland Asia would show up as the lowest branches of the tree. Languages spoken on islands sequentially farther out would appear in correspondingly higher branches.

Jordan and her colleagues used statistical methods to map the proposed migrations onto the language tree. They found that the languages of islands near Asia split off on lower boughs of the tree than did languages spoken on islands farther out. The result was a nearly optimal fit, says Jordan. "It would require a very different tree to disagree with the express train," she adds.

"The archaeological evidence shows a clear historical pattern" of how Pacific people spread, says Patrick V. Kirch, director of the Hearst Museum of Anthropology at the University of California, Berkeley. "When we get similar results from archaeology, traditional linguistics, and now this, it tells us we're really onto something."

Though the number of researchers applying phylogenetic techniques to languages is small, the idea is spreading. At a conference last March, Pagel presented his team's ongoing study, which is using complex models of evolution to build trees. His preliminary results support many of the existing theories of relationships among the Indo-European languages.

The tree shows some ancient linguistic splits that would be difficult to reconstruct using traditional linguistic-tree building, says Pagel. For example, Greek appears to be one of the first languages to branch off the European bough. "Everything we know about archeology tells us [Greek] is very old," he says, "combined with the fact that no one else can understand a word of it and that it has a different alphabet."

Trees or Nets?

Despite the apparent success of the method so far, many academics are cautious about examining languages by using methods developed for biological species. They point out an important difference. Biological traits only rarely transfer between individuals of the same generation or unrelated lineages.

Although small amounts of DNA move between species, languages undergo far more mixing. For example, English is Germanic in origin, but the Norman invasion of England in the 11th century resulted in many French terms joining the language. Similarly in recent times, Japanese has acquired many English words, including commercial and technological terms. This is akin to a lineage of bears somehow acquiring the beak of a duck.

Most "species by definition can't borrow evolutionary features . . . while in linguistic or cultural contexts, such borrowings are perfectly possible," says Scott MacEachern, an archaeologist at Bowdoin College in Brunswick, Maine. The language-tree researchers assume isolated communities, continues MacEachern. This is not how groups normally behave, he says.

There's no reason why language, genes, and culture should evolve in the same ways, agrees John E. Terrell, an anthropologist at the Field Museum in Chicago. "There is nothing equivalent to genetic isolation in languages," he says. Because languages frequently transfer words or phrases between lineages, their relationships might more accurately be depicted as a net than a tree.

However, he concedes, applying the biological phylogenetic approach to languages "can be used to produce a first approximation [of lingual relationships] as long as you never lose sight that it's a quick-and-dirty technique."

Language trees may become more quickly accepted for specific sorts of broad-brushstroke studies, such as questions of large-scale colonization over long periods.

Although many "anthropologists are horrified at the thought of treating cultural groups as bounded units evolving through time," says Monique Borgerhoff Mulder, an anthropologist at the University of California, Davis, they're "missing the scale of the question." She argues, "Specific mechanisms of social change are not relevant at this scale."

Even those who advocate phylogenetic methods to build language trees admit that the sharing of words between languages is a problem. However, some words are subject to less exchange than others. Pagel suggests that by avoiding technological terms and other language elements that are frequently transferred, the language-tree method can become more useful.

The technique holds too much promise to dismiss, says Gray. He points to its potential to foster synergism among biology, anthropology, archaeology, and linguistics. "Instead of different disciplines thinking that they have the golden bullet . . . we need to tie everything together," he says.

Researchers and computer programmers have been toying with the concept of "virtual organisms" for decades. For much of this time, their focus has been on creating artificial intelligence—computers that can learn from experience and think on their own without the

aid of a programmer or operator. The results have been mixed, largely because human thought processes are difficult to mimic or program, affected as they are by so many nonrational variables (such as emotions, memories, intuition, desire, etc.). According to this Dallas Morning News *article, however, computers do have something to teach us about evolution, particularly the emergence of complex organisms from very simple origins. As a result, many evolutionary theorists are turning to computers to gain insight into the same adaptive processes that shaped our own hearts and brains. This type of interdisciplinary work is possible because the basic rules of natural selection are reasonably straightforward: there must be variation, that variation must be inheritable, and different variants must have different fitness.* —KH

"Computer 'Life' Explains Evolution of Complexity"
by Tom Siegfried
Dallas Morning News, May 12, 2003

Life started out small and gradually got bigger. Computers were born big and have been shrinking ever since.

But both life and computers began simple, growing more complex as they evolved. You can argue about which one is winning the complexity race—nowadays, whether computer circuitry or the human brain is more complicated depends on whose brain you're comparing to which computer.

Of course, computer complexity has progressed thanks to clever programmers and chipmakers, so humankind can still claim a sort of complexity superiority. But computers may offer the people the clues needed to solve the mystery of how life got to be so complex.

In particular, "organs of extreme perfection and complication," in Charles Darwin's words, don't self-materialize spontaneously out of some primordial slime. Darwin suggested that features such as eyes must have evolved piecemeal. Simpler features must have been transformed into complex organs by small changes accumulating over countless generations of offspring.

Plenty of evidence supports Darwin's suspicion, but it's not easy to demonstrate it in detail. Fossils are merely random snapshots. What you need is long-term time-lapse photography. But that's where computers can help. Self-replicating software called "digital organisms" can reproduce and evolve over thousands of generations with every event recorded for analysis. Such "virtual evolution" can show how complexity arises.

"Digital organisms undergo the same processes of reproduction, mutation, inheritance and competition that allow evolution and adaptation by natural selection in organic forms," scientists from Michigan State University and the California Institute of Technology write in the current issue of the journal *Nature*.

Digital organisms are similar to computer viruses, which replicate by co-opting the resources of a "host" computer. You can just as easily write programs that reproduce on their own, kind of like bacteria, by simply copying their "genome," or set of instructions.

The question is, can such a self-replicating program evolve into something more elaborate, with greater capabilities and complexities? The answer is yes, the scientists reported.

Using software called Avida, they performed experiments showing how digital organisms could evolve in a computer "environment." Each program-organism begins with a "genome" consisting of 50 instruction steps—each step designated to execute one of 26 possible instructions. To conduct the digital equivalent of metabolism, each organism has a small memory space for accepting input from the "environment" and computing "output."

For example, the input could be two lists of 32 bits— 0s and 1s. The instructions in the digital genome would then process the input lists to produce a new 32-bit string for output. An organism performing logic functions could manipulate the input strings in different ways— writing a 1 where both strings had the same digit, for example, and writing 0 where the input strings differed.

The digital organisms also need the equivalent of food—or "energy units." A program that evolves the ability to do logic functions gets more energy, allowing it to reproduce more rapidly.

At the start, all the organisms get enough energy to reproduce, but only one of the 26 instruction options performs logic (the NAND, or "not and," instruction familiar to all programmers). Combined properly with other instructions, the NAND ability can perform additional logic functions for more sophisticated processing.

With only NAND for starters, though, a digital organism can't do any fancy processing. Its progeny might, though, because reproduction isn't perfect. Mutations (errors in the copying) can occur—deleting, altering or duplicating one of the 50 instruction steps. Most of the time such a change wrecks the program so it can't reproduce itself (so it dies). But sometimes the change provides a new mix of instructions permitting higher-level logic. A new function wins more "energy" and leads to more reproduction, with more chances for new mutations that can lead to new abilities.

A particularly sophisticated ability is the EQU function (for "equals"). To perform it, the organism must compare the 32 bits in two input strings and then write a 1 for each position where the digits are equal (both 0 or both 1) and a 0 at each position where the input strings differ. From 50 populations, each consisting of 3,600 identical copies of an ancestral digital organism, progeny of 23 evolved the ability to perform the EQU function.

"Our experiments demonstrate the validity of the hypothesis, first articulated by Darwin . . . that complex features generally evolve by modifying existing structures and functions," write Richard Lenski, Charles Ofria and Robert Pennock of Michigan State and Christoph Adami of Caltech.

Many different combinations of mutations produced organisms that were equal to the EQU task. All the lineages that could do it first produced simpler logic functions, although no one simpler function was essential to EQU.

Perhaps most intriguing, one of the digital organism lineages evolved a way to do EQU with only 17 instructions. Beforehand, the best the humans could do was write out a program to do EQU requiring 19 instructions.

In other words, there are many pathways to the EQU ability—and no one royal evolutionary road to complexity. Computers and people can both be complex, and evolve whatever way works for them.

Reprinted with permission of the Dallas Morning News.

Web Sites

Due to the changing nature of Internet links, the Rosen Publishing Group, Inc., has developed an online list of Web sites related to the subject of this book. This site is updated regularly. Please use this link to access the list:

http://www.rosenlinks.com/cdfb/biev

For Further Reading

Barlow, Connie. *The Ghosts of Evolution: Nonsensical Fruit, Missing Partners, and Other Ecological Anachronisms*. New York, NY: Basic Books, 2002.

Cartwright, John. *Evolution and Human Behavior*. Cambridge, MA: Bradford Books, 2000.

Dawkins, Richard. *The Selfish Gene*. New York, NY: Oxford University Press, 1990.

Diamond, Jared M. *The Third Chimpanzee: The Evolution and Future of the Human Animal*. New York, NY: HarperPerennial, 1992.

Gould, Stephen Jay. *The Structure of Evolutionary Theory*. Cambridge, MA: Belknap Press, 2002.

Jones, Stephen, ed. *The Cambridge Encyclopedia of Human Evolution*. New York, NY: Cambridge University Press, 1994.

Larson, Edward J. *Evolution: The Remarkable History of a Scientific Theory*. New York, NY: Modern Library, 2004.

Mayr, Ernst. *What Evolution Is*. New York, NY: Basic Books, 2002.

Tattersall, Ian. *Becoming Human: Evolution and Human Uniqueness*. New York, NY: Harvest Books, 1999.

Zimmer, Carl. *Evolution: The Triumph of an Idea*. New York, NY: HarperPerennial, 2002.

Bibliography

Gorner, Peter. "New Genetic Techniques Show Deadly Evolution of SARS Virus." *Chicago Tribune*, January 30, 2004.

Guterman, Lila. "Trapped by Evolution: Animals' Instincts Lead Them Astray in Modern, Much-Altered Environments." *Chronicle of Higher Education*, October 18, 2002, pp. A19–A20.

Harder, Ben. "The Seeds of Malaria: Recent Evolution Cultivated a Deadly Scourge." *Science News*, Vol. 160, No. 19, November 10, 2001, pp. 296–298.

Hayden, Thomas, Jessica Ruvinsky, Dan Gilgoff, and Rachel K. Sobel. "A Theory Evolves." *U.S. News and World Report*, Vol. 133, No. 4, July 29, 2002, p. 43.

Holmes, Bob. "Ready, Steady, Evolve." *New Scientist*, Vol. 175, No. 2362, September 28, 2002, pp. 28–31.

Kerr, Richard A. "New Mammal Data Challenge Evolutionary Pulse Theory." *Science*, Vol. 273, No. 5274, July 26, 1996, pp. 431–432.

Laland, Kevin, and John Odling-Smee. "Life's Little Builders." *New Scientist*, Vol. 180 No. 2421, pp. 42–45, November 15, 2003, p. 42.

Lawton, Graham. "Here Be Monsters." *New Scientist*, Vol. 167, No. 2257, September 23, 2000, p. 22.

Pickrell, John. "Searching for the Tree of Babel: Linguistic Evolution May Shed Light on History." *Science News*, Vol. 161, No. 21, May 25, 2002, pp. 328–329.

Raloff, Janet. "Dying Breeds: Livestock Are Developing a Largely Unrecognized Biodiversity Crisis." *Science News*, Vol. 152, No. 14, October 4, 1997, pp. 216–218.

Randerson, James. "Together We Are Stronger." *New Scientist*, Vol. 177, No. 2386, March 15, 2003, pp. 1–4.

Shine, R., B. Phillips, H. Waye, M. LeMaster, and R. T. Mason. "Benefits of Female Mimicry in Snakes." *Nature*, Vol. 414, No. 6861, November 15, 2001, p. 267.

Siegfried, Tom. "Computer 'Life' Explains Evolution of Complexity." *Dallas Morning News*, May 12, 2003.

Stanford University Medical Center. "Stanford Research Points to Chance as Cause of Genetic Diseases in Ashkenazi Jews." News release, February 27, 2003.

Stewart, Ian. "How the Species Became." *New Scientist*, Vol. 180, No. 2416, October 11, 2003, pp. 32–35.

Summers, Adam. "Uphill Flight: A Partridge's Ability to Climb Overhanging Slopes Might Explain How Dinosaurs Took to the Skies." *Natural History*, Vol. 112, No. 10, December 2003, pp. 30–31.

Wade, Nicholas. "Miniature People Add Extra Pieces to Evolutionary Puzzle." *New York Times*, November 9, 2004.

Wade, Nicholas. "Staple of Evolutionary Teaching May Not Be Textbook Case." *New York Times*, June 18, 2002.

Witze, Alexandra. "Scientists Question Whether Humans Caused Extinction of Mammoths." *Dallas Morning News*, September 25, 2003.

Yoon, Carol Kaesuk. "The Evolving Peppered Moth Gains a Furry Counterpart." *New York Times*, June 17, 2003.

Index

About the Editor

Katy Human writes about science for the *Denver Post* newspaper, covering everything from space science to wildlife research. Human has a Ph.D. in ecology from Stanford University, and has been fascinated by ecology and evolution since her childhood, when she spent days in the Smithsonian's Natural History Museum in Washington, D.C. She's been a journalist since 1997.

Photo Credits

Front Cover: (Top, left inset) © Inmagine.com; (bottom left) © Pixtal/Superstock; (background) © Royalty Free/Corbis; (lower right inset) © Pascal Goetgheluck/Photo Researchers, Inc.; Back Cover: (bottom inset) © Inmagine.com; (top) © Royalty Free/Corbis.

Designer: Geri Fletcher